What Kind of God?

Margaret Kane

WHAT KIND OF GOD?

*Reflections on Working with People and
Churches in North-East England*

SCM PRESS LTD

British Library Cataloguing in Publication Data

Kane, Margaret
    What kind of God?: reflections on working
    with people and churches in North-east
    England.
    1. Christian Life
    I. Title
    248.4   BV4501.2

    ISBN 0–334–01770–X

First published 1986
by SCM Press Ltd
26–30 Tottenham Road, London N1

Typeset at the Spartan Press Ltd
Lymington, Hants
and printed in Great Britain by
Richard Clay (The Chaucer Press) Ltd
Bungay, Suffolk

I offer this book
as a token of thanks to
David Jenkins
Robert Moore
    and
to the memory of
John Loftus
who together acted as my
Advisory Group
from 1969–1981

Contents

I   How God got Hold of Me

1. Who is this woman? Where has she sprung from? What right
has she to offer these views to the church about its life and
mission? What are her credentials?

Christian theology is essentially testimony. We can only
proclaim 'that which we have seen and heard' (I John 1.3). When
in 1969 I arrived in North-East England to take up the post of
Theological Consultant, few people knew anything about me. It
was natural that they should ask what right I had to offer my
particular insights and upon what authority they were based.
This brief autobiographical note aims to answer that question. It
does not do this by describing the processes of thought by which I
arrived at certain conclusions about God, but by giving an
account of events which were not planned by me, and which
followed a course which I could not have foreseen. It is an
account not of how I found God but of how God got hold of me.

I was brought up in a Christian home and as a child there was
no question in my mind about the reality of God. As I grew up
other things seemed more important. Going to school meant
adapting to people who had different outlooks and values.

In my early teens one set of girls who had an evangelical
enthusiasm affected my thinking about God. Through them the
Rev. Bryan Green was invited to preach at the school. This led to a
mini-revival, the chief expression of which was that people began
passing the marmalade at breakfast rather than leaving you to
grab it as best you could! Individuals were nobbled and walked
round the games field being interrogated about their souls 'Are
you saved?' I went along without enthusiasm with this outbreak
of religion, though I found it extremely childish.

When I left school one of these girls was in digs near mine in
London. She was studying medicine at London University and
was a member of the London Inter-Faculty Christian Union
(LIFCU). She invited me to some of their 'squashes'. Many of the

discussions were memorable for their silliness 'Should a Christian girl wear a yellow polo-necked jumper – or is she not thereby
simply trying to attract the opposite sex?' 'It is wrong to dance
(which I enjoyed) – think how your bodies are pressed together!'
Evolution was disproved by an involved use of biblical texts.
There were tremendous strengths in this group. A discipline in
prayer with a 'quiet hour' before breakfast each day and a sense
that the whole of life had to be committed to God. But the general
effect of their 'package' was personally inhibiting and life
denying. I wanted a God who was liberating and life-affirming.
So I broke away.

But God does make absolute claims, and this I discovered in
another way. I was at the Art School and enjoying life immensely.
When Lent came I suggested to my friend that we ought to do
something 'Let's go to church at lunch time each day'.

On the first day she came with me, but on the second day I
went alone. Near to Regent Street Polytechnic Art School is All
Souls' Church, Langham Place. I went into the dark church and
knelt down. Then – a conviction came to me, like a bolt from the
blue 'You've got to be a missionary'. I knew nothing about
missionaries but what I had seen on slides in the village hall.
Nothing was further from my mind. But God was confronting me
with his absolute demand, his personal claim upon my whole
life. I had no doubt about the urgency and reality of this demand.
It was impossible to ignore or disobey it.

I did not go back to the Art School that afternoon, but walked
round the streets of London, screwing up my courage to tell my
parents about my proposed change of direction (I had already
shocked them by refusing the place I had gained at London
University to read chemistry and maths). The next week I
searched out the Church Missionary Society's offices and went to
see the candidate's secretary. Sitting in the waiting room I was
not helped by the picture on the wall under which was the
caption 'Who chooses me must give and hazard all he hath'. It
was not really necessary to rub it in! But I was quite clear that I
must go through with it, and had no thought of ducking out.

I do not know what I expected of the interview, but what I got
brought me down to earth in no uncertain way. Being a
missionary was seen by this woman as being a teacher and going
to their teachers' training college. She asked me why I was not
happy about what she proposed, and I stumblingly said 'Well I
thought I was doing something (in the Art School) first-rate and

what you suggest sounds second-rate'. What she made of that I do not know, but she ended by giving me some very dull looking study notes and said 'Work on these and come and see me again sometime'.

I was out of my depth. I took the notes reluctantly and went back to my digs. The notes were there accusing me of half-heartedness. Life, as it had been before this upset, looked good and re-assuring. I opened the bottom drawer of my dressing table and stuffed the notes in underneath everything else. Perhaps they would rise up and challenge me, perhaps, if I were foolhardy enough to go anywhere near the CMS offices, someone would rush out and drag me in, but perhaps this would be the end of the affair. I returned to my carefree life and did not mention the matter again. It is possible to say 'No' to God.

But even if we turn against God, God is faithful to us. A varied social life continued in London during the week, and at home at week-ends. I had enough friends of both sexes not to be alert to a growing affection between myself and a married man. This 'unsuitable' attachment should not be seen as a negative experience with no other purpose than to bring me back to God. In this man, who was totally unconnected with the church or 'religion', I found things that had been missing in my 'Godly' contacts, an affirmation of life, the ability to value and to derive fun from very ordinary things, and a generous love of people. Though his education had been far less 'privileged' than mine, he was shocked at my ignorance and persuaded me to read the papers and to look forward to having a vote when I was twenty-one. Neither of us saw the danger signs until we were deeply involved. Then we struggled without much success to get back to a normal relationship. The whole thing was agonizing and long drawn out. Seeing no end to the torment and no possible way out, I began to cry out to God – 'God, you must do something!'

God answered my prayer. A friend of mine who had left the Art School invited me to meet her at lunchtime one day. We went to Hampstead Heath, where we sat on a bench eating our sandwiches. It was some weeks since I had seen her and she told me that she had been helping at a Settlement run by some women of deep Christian conviction. As she described the activities of the Settlement she said 'I have come to the conclusion that either these women are mad or everyone else is mad. I think they are right'. As she said these words it was as if I heard God saying to me 'Now or never! This is your last chance'. I was completely terror-struck. I felt the desolation and futility of life without God. It was hell. I could face anything rather than that. In my heart I said 'Yes! Yes God, I will, I'll do anything you want, but don't leave me'. Outwardly my friend and I went on with our conversation and she was unaware that anything special had happened to me. Back at the Art School I went immediately to the basement cloakroom, the only place where I could be alone. In the darkness with the coats hanging all around, I leant against the dirty windows and prayed, 'I promise you God I will do whatever you say. I won't hold anything back'.

There was no thought now of being a missionary. I had come to realize that God is to be served in ordinary matters. This was not to be achieved by 'once for all sacrifices', but by a slow process of being alert to and responding to each opportunity as it presented itself. All I knew was that I must pray and wait and be prepared to take the next step. In the basement of the hostel where I lodged during the week, there was a small dark room, set aside I think for a quiet room, but completely unused. As I shared a bedroom with another girl I resorted to this room each evening and prayed. I wished there was someone to help me, but for a long time I was alone in my fumbling. Then one day a woman at the hostel introduced me to the parish priest of a nearby church.

He realized that I needed more than soothing words, took my searchings seriously, and for some weeks gave me individual instruction in Christian faith. I started going to the church, went to my first silent retreat and before long made my first confession. This was a mile-stone for me in that I felt I was freed from the past. In all this I was becoming less dependent on my own feelings and finding solid ground in belief and practice within a church fellowship. I even bought my first theological book (*An Outline of the Old Testament* by Povah).

My instruction left me in no doubt about God's concern with the world. I read the Left Book Club publications that were coming out at the time, joined the Peace Pledge Union, befriended some German Jewish refugees and got involved in questions of unemployment. One day the priest said to me 'You have spent enough time thinking about yourself. You should now do something for other people. Will you help with the girls' club?'

I have described elsewhere the effect my involvement with the girl's club had upon me. In the contrast between the unbelief of these disadvantaged young people and my belief the yawning

gap that exists between Christian faith and the majority of people
was forced upon my attention:

> None of the girls attended church. I do not think they had
> even been inside it. It seemed that there was a total separation
> between Christian faith as it was understood by those who
> worshipped in the upstairs church and life as it was experi-
> enced by the girls in the downstairs club.
>
> Yet Christian faith is about the offer of life, and that is what
> these girls wanted. Given a chance, they would opt for life, but
> the upstairs church did not present them with a viable option.
> And when it came to the point – when the question 'What is it
> all about?' was directed at me – I was unable to say anything.
>
> My inability to make any sort of response was one of the
> causes that set me on to a search for some way of helping
> people to discover a faith that bites on the actual circumstances
> of their lives. [1]

If I were to pursue this search I needed two things: to
understand my own faith in greater depth, so that I could
respond flexibly to the varied needs of others, rather than offer
them my own 'package'; and to get closer to the people to whom I
wished to minister, especially those who are most disadvantaged. These people it seems to me are excluded from Christian
faith, not by their own choice, but by reason of a cultural gap. I
wanted to be *there* with them on their side of the gap.

During this time my own life was becoming somewhat
schizoid. In the day I was working as an artist in Bond Street,
advertising luxury beauty products. At night I was at the girls'
club in a back street near King's Cross station. Tension between
the two sides of my life increased and I began to apply for jobs as a
youth leader. After being turned down several times on account
of my lack of training, I realized that I was not going to get
anywhere until I got some training. But what kind of training? I
was now aware that the question I was asking about the gospel
affected not only young people but our whole society. I received
conflicting advice about training and opted for the proposal that I
should work at a settlement in London while studying for a
Theological Diploma, but just before I was due to go to the
settlement it was bombed out of existence. As a result, without
any idea of what it might lead to, I went to a theological college for
two years, so entering the formal process of becoming an
accredited church worker.

I am immensely grateful for all I learnt during those two years. There are, however dangers in becoming a 'professional' minister. The danger to which I was most exposed, but of which I was unaware for some time, was that of allowing the aims and values of the institutional church to divert me from my true calling to minister to people who are estranged from the church.

I will briefly fill in the next few years. Before leaving College interviews were arranged for me in a number of parishes in and around London. There didn't seem to be much to choose between them and I landed up in a parish in London 'over the border'. Nationally the church was appealing for women to work as Chaplains' Assistants with women in the Forces and I thought that would suit me, but was told that I must first have some parish experience. Within a year, however, the Bishop of Chelmsford asked my Rector to release me for that work. This put me in touch again with the people I wanted to serve and in war and post-war conditions it gave me valuable experience which I needed. When demobilization got under way I felt it was time that I too returned to 'civvy street', and I went again to a parish, this time in Birmingham. Here my experience was less positive.

It was my day off. I rode my bike to the outskirts of the city, found a field and sat in it all day reading. The book I was reading was *Revolution in a City Parish* by Abbé Michonneau. In it the Abbé described his working-class parish in Paris:

> We are confronted by a pagan proletariat . . . the mentality of their surroundings completely conquers them. . . . Our mission must aim, not to organize those who already are practising Catholics . . . but to penetrate the different milieux with the Spirit of Christianity.[2]

He emphasized a point made by another writer concerned with the same situation:

> It is not individuals only that must be christianized, it is the society also, the institutions, the manners and customs.[3]

I was already familiar with other French mission movements including that of the Worker Priests. The problem they faced was not that people had no need of God, but that they were excluded from hearing the gospel by sociological and cultural barriers. Abbé Godin wrote of the hunger of young workers for God:

Two, three, four or more times, sometimes over a period of years God calls these young proletarians in the depths of their souls. . . . The Christian possibilities of these pagans are greater than we conceive . . . the difficulty lies in finding the best road for them and then in affiliating them with, or making them into, a Christian community.[4]

The parish I was working in was in a suburban part of Birmingham. There were people in it who were poor and deprived, and I met them in their homes in my parish visiting. I remember the woman who took in lodgers, who told me that she did not know even the name of the father of her youngest child; the eight children of another family who rushed in from school to be given thick slices of bread cut on the bare table and spread with jam; and the old people out of whose cracked cups I drank tea. The parish church had a growing congregation many of whom came from the professions and business. Few of the poorer people came to church and if they did they entered an alien world in which they were not fully themselves. What they received there was not sufficient to change their outlook on life. To quote Michonneau again 'The anti-religious, or rather pagan attitude is so strong . . . that the mentality of those who have been baptized, and whom some would like to call "real Christians", is no different from that of the non-baptized. The conduct of both is the same. We can consider both as pagans'.[5] I did not see that visiting on its own could achieve much.

I was beginning to become painfully aware that I was being deflected from what I believed to be my true calling – to reach with the gospel people who are at present outside the influence of the church. I felt deeply for the young workers mentioned by Abbé Godin. I knew from my own experience how disturbing it is to feel God moving you in the depths of your being yet being unable to respond. I was reminded of how the girls in the club in London stood on the other side of a gap that separated them from faith in God. It was these experiences that had led me to become a full-time church worker; but now I seemed to be getting off course.

Apart from the French pioneers, the only person I knew who was thinking along the same lines as myself was the Bishop of Sheffield, Leslie Hunter, whom I had met at a church workers' meeting in London. At that time he had suggested that I might work in his Diocese, but I had not followed this up as I had only just gone to the Birmingham parish. Now I did not know what to do – so I did nothing. In the end it was the vicar who asked me to move. He probably sensed my restlessness and as another suitable worker had become available he decided to bring matters to a head. As I was still not clear what to do, I spent two terms at William Temple College, which at that time was at Hawarden, and, with the help of Mollie Batten the Principal, began to clear my thoughts and see what the possibilities were. In the end the choice was easy and I spent the next fourteen years in the Sheffield Diocese. This was a great experience, for under the leadership of Bishop Hunter the whole Diocese was geared towards mission in an industrial society.[6] I spent the first seven years in the mining parish of Maltby, where I was responsible for building up Christian community in a new area. In the process I got to know miners, their families and the issues of a mining community. The first stage of this task was over with the completion of a church building in the area, and I left Maltby to become for the next seven years a chaplain of the Sheffield Industrial Mission. In both jobs I felt that I was getting back 'on course'. In the Industrial Mission especially I knew that at last I could give all my time to people who were on the other side of the gap.

One typical place I visited was a large workshop in which about two hundred men were making machine tools. These were highly skilled men working on one-off jobs. On one occasion, as I stopped by a man's machine the myth that all factory jobs are boring was exploded as he turned to me and said '*Your* job must be boring!'

To begin with I was just a novelty and they watched to see how long I would survive. When it became clear that I was surviving they began to talk more freely. Their attitude was one of deep cynicism, about people, and institutions – management, unions and not least the church. 'Everyone is out for themselves; it all boils down to self-interest.' About their own place in life they were fatalistic for they saw that that had been settled once and for all when they first 'put on overalls'.

Their question was not so much 'Is there a God?' as 'Is that God worth believing in?' In view of the state of the world it seemed to them that God was either powerless or immoral in allowing things to go on as they were.

I began to introduce topics of conversation that, coming from a church worker, surprised them: automation, young people at work, immigration. My aim was to break into their set pattern of thinking, so that space could be made for new ideas. Conversations with groups or individuals tended to go in one of two directions: towards a social concern – for instance when a steel melter began to realize that he was not the only person affected by changes at his works; or towards a personal concern – for instance when one man unexpectedly said to me 'I now believe in God. What do I do next?'

With individuals I followed up whatever questions they raised, but in the more public conversations I stuck to a discussion about what was going on in their experience at work and beyond. In doing this I was in no way avoiding talk of the gospel, rather I was opening up the area with which the gospel is concerned and upon which questions about God could be tackled.

If Christian faith is to be presented as a point of view about life and as a way of life for people in these circumstances and with this background of misunderstanding and unbelief, theological insights and skills of a high order are required. These insights and skills I had set myself to acquire.

The communication of the gospel in today's world was also a matter of concern to I. T. Ramsey, whom I met while I was in Sheffield and he was a Professor of Theology at Oxford. When he became Bishop of Durham in 1966 he remembered our meeting and invited me to work with him in North-East England. I was not able to take up the offer until 1969, for disagreements in the Sheffield Mission had already led me to accept a short term job to start Industrial Mission at the invitation of the Christian Council in Hong Kong.

My time in Hong Kong helped me to see my search in an international context. Hong Kong in 1966, through its rapid transformation, represented the typical industrialized society. So speedy were the changes that one could observe, not only the changing skyline as new skyscrapers and factories were built, but the changing attitudes of people. Only the older people clung to their traditional religions. The younger people discarded them as inadequate to meet the questions of this kind of world, and moved to a state of agnosticism or to a private interiorized religion that was unconcerned with what was happening in the world. My job was to get Industrial Mission started and this meant finding entry points for work, tapping sources of finance, finding staff and other practicalities. I was conscious that my over busy-ness left little time for tackling the main question of how belief in God is possible in a technological society. Yet this fundamental theological task had to be tackled, and this I looked forward to doing when I returned to England.

2. The story that runs through this book starts at the point when I took up the post of Theological Consultant in North-East England. The purpose of the book is not to tell my story but to reflect on what, in the process of these events, I have learnt about God. Because I believe that our understanding of God, that is our theology, starts at the point where God meets us in life, narrative and theology are inter-woven. At this point, if my argument is to be intelligible, I need to fill in the background of events out of which the theology emerged.

My next meeting with Ian Ramsey was in May 1969 immediately after my return from Hong Kong. This time we met in the Chapter House in Durham Cathedral, a cold gothic vestibule in contrast with the book-lined Oxford study of our previous meeting. A hard-pressed bishop is different from an Oxford don. It was obvious that the bishop was short of time and unprepared to enter into much discussion about the exact nature of the job he wanted me to do as a 'theological consultant'. I too had changed and my ideas had developed. I caught his interest by my enthusiasm for the kind of job that the Church of Scotland was offering at that time for someone to work in the field of science, religion and technology. I thought this concept might be the focus of an ecumenical theological enterprise throughout the North-East Region. He asked me to draw up a job description on these lines (see Appendix I), and to start work as soon as I was ready. Then he hurried away.

Many aspects of the job remained unclear, but it seemed to me that these would have to be worked out on the job. After further correspondence I accepted the post and on 1 July 1969 I took up the appointment as Theological Consultant in North-East England. Bishop Ian was anxious that work should be done ecumenically and regionally. He therefore consulted the North-East Ecumenical Group, which is a non-executive body that brings together the church leaders of the region. Money for salary and expenses was provided by Durham Diocese, while Newcastle Diocese paid for my housing. Later York Diocese covered the expenses for work done in that Diocese.

It was left to me to decide where to live. A number of factors, not least the availability of a council flat, led me to settle in Billingham, which is about mid-way between the Northern and Southern extremes of the area I was to cover.

Bishop Ramsey had a vision of a church that would look outwards to help people find and respond to God in the world. This demanded a radical change of stance on the part of the church. To be concerned with the world means working ecumenically and regionally (hence the formation of the North-East Ecumenical Group). Above all it requires a new theological perspective. It was to help this process of change that he appointed me as 'theological consultant'. Again it was left to me to decide the shape and focus of the job and to give content to that title.

My approach to the task was shaped by my understanding of theology. The word 'theology' means 'the science of God' – so that drives one back to one's understanding of God. Some people see God – and therefore theology – as detached from everyday life. My belief is that God is creator, redeemer and inspirer of all that is. Hence for me theology is an understanding of life from the perspective of faith in God. It follows that my concern as theological consultant would have to be with every aspect of the region's life.

At its best the church has always been concerned with the whole of life, but the conditions for exercising this kind of ministry have changed:

> In the past the churches expressed their proper concern with the whole of life through parish and congregational structures. By these means the influence of the local churches spread out naturally in all directions. But in today's extremely complex society these traditional structures can only deal with a limited number of human activities. They can no longer express the original intention of concern with the whole of life. This function can now be fulfilled only if the churches base their action on zonal or regional levels.[7]

The North-East Region of England is in many ways a natural *zone humaine*, that is to say that for many people most aspects of their lives are expressed within the region.[8] I have said a good deal about North-East England in my earlier books.[9] Here I will confine my remarks to changes that have taken place in the last few years.

Unemployment is the biggest issue in the region. In 1978 unemployment in the Northern Region was 9.3% against 6.2% in Great Britain as a whole.[10] In 1984 the region's unemployment was 19.1%, the highest in Britain. Today within the region,

Cleveland has the doubtful distinction of having the highest
unemployment rate of 25%. The gap between the better-off
regions and the North has widened. Northumberland, Tyne and
Wear, Durham and Cleveland are in the bottom 12 out of 131
regions in Europe.

Heavy industry has continued to decline. The Region's
steel-making industries continue to be severely affected. In coal
mining, of the 4 million tonnes that were scheduled to be cut from
production nationally in 1984, one third (1.4 million tonnes) was
earmarked for the North-East coalfield – the highest drop (12%)
of any region. Now in 1986 in the North East, where pits used to
be numbered in hundreds, operating pits have been reduced to
only *nine*. In the construction industry the increase in orders
between 1982 and 1983 was only half that in the nation as a whole.

But it is not only the traditional heavy industries that are
shedding labour. The chemical industry, which since the end of
World War I has given hope and stable employment to thousands
of people in Cleveland, has in recent years drastically reduced its
work force. In the face of cut-throat competition and changing
processes, products and markets, it is forced to continue to
replace labour by new capital investment, and the 20,000 people
it employed in 1980 is now less than half that number.[11] Even
then its very survival remains under threat.

Unemployment in the past tended to be more or less short-
term, but today there are many long-term unemployed people. A
quarter of the unemployed young people aged sixteen to
nineteen have been out of work for more than a year. Many
people both old and young, have given up hope of ever having a
job again.

It is not surprising that the Northern Region has the highest
rate of population decline of any region – a 2.6% drop compared
with 1.5% growth in England as a whole. 12,000 more people are
leaving the region than are coming in every year. 40% of those
who leave are aged between seventeen and twenty-eight years.

The danger is that the old image of the North of England as a
depressed and depressing region will return. High-flyers, who
can choose where to work, will not come into the region, and
even ICI, which in the past has brought many able people to
Cleveland, has in the last year recruited no graduates at all.

Poverty is once again a real problem in the North. The Region
has the lowest household income in the whole country. One
household in every six has an average weekly income of less than

fifty pounds. Educational aspirations and results, with regard for instance, to the percentage of children staying on at school after the statutory minimum leaving age of sixteen, the proportion going on to full-time further education and the numbers leaving with graded results, compares unfavourably with the national average and so on.

To make matters worse there is increasing division between the employed and the unemployed. The paradox is that where one member of the family is employed it is quite often the case that a second member also has a job, while in other families there is no wage-earner at all. Where husband and wife are both working there is undreamed of wealth. So in our increasingly divided society, there are not only the obvious divisions between North and South, but divisions within the region itself.

Of course there are some hopeful signs. There is an increase in the number of small firms and of people setting up their own companies perhaps with redundancy money. This is a big change in an area which has until now been dependent on large companies for employment. But the formation of small firms continues to be the lowest of any region, and self-employment is the lowest in the country (6.9% of total employment compared with 8.9% nationally).

A number of new firms have come into the region, for instance on the reclaimed land around the mouth of the Tees, where a number of petro-chemical firms have been set up. Before we hail these as the hope of the future several features need to be noted. First, these firms are capital-intensive and employ comparatively few workers. One million pounds worth of investment *may* produce just one job. Secondly they are branches of foreign-owned multi-national corporations, which means that their control is not in the hands of local people. Many have their headquarters in the United States, but others including the Nissan car factory now being built at Washington in the County of Tyne and Wear, are based in Japan. Thirdly, technological change is now so rapid that many new plants have a very short life span. This affects not only the foreign companies, but new companies that have come into being in response to the require-ments of North Sea Oil. The oil rig construction companies can for instance only last as long as oil extraction continues – a time estimated at not more than fifteen years. I have mentioned technological change before,[12] the new thing is its increased rapidity. Sophisticated new plant is obsolescent even before it has been erected, and brave attempts by local councils and others to landscape and restore waste land cannot keep up with the continuing process of demolition.

The general effect of Central Government Policy is to make things worse. Direct Government support for industry since 1981/2 has been cut back by 50%. Spending on Regional policy has declined steadily, and of what remains Scotland and Wales receive an increasing share of the total, largely because of their Development Agency status. [13]

Cuts in social services and all types of benefits hit hardest at those who are already disadvantaged and that goes for the whole region. The impression is given that as far as Central Government is concerned it neither knows nor cares about what is happening in the North and that for them the North is best forgotten.

It is surprising that there has been little protest about all this. It seems that people in the North are so used to being among the most disadvantaged that they expect nothing better. It is true that there are some signs particularly in the mining communities, of a more confrontational style of politics, but most people, including those with authority in local government and trade unions, are working on the assumption that in time full employment will be restored and things will return to 'normal'. It would, I think, be more realistic to recognize that the economy of the region has totally collapsed, that there is no possibility of going back and that there must be a different kind of future.

I have much to say later about how the church is reacting to these changes in society. At this point I confine myself to changes that took place in the internal affairs of the churches which had considerable effect on my work. The first big change was when in April 1972 Bishop Ian had a heart attack, had six months off work and then in October of that year, soon after his return to work, died.

In 1973 John Habgood was appointed Bishop of Durham, where he remained until he became Archbishop of York in 1983. There were also changes among the other church leaders to whom I related. A new Bishop of Newcastle was appointed in 1972 and again in 1981, and a new Archbishop of York in 1976. Changes in the other denominations included the Chairman of both Methodist Districts and the Roman Catholic Bishop of Middlesbrough.

In growing into the job I was extraordinarily fortunate in the members of my advisory group. I realized from the start that I could not do the job without help. Bishop Ramsey was always ready to respond to specific requests for help, but he was too busy to give thought to the detailed planning of the job. I therefore invited three people to be an informal advisory group. The group consisted of Canon David Jenkins, Director of the World Council of Churches Humanum Programme, Rev. John Loftus, Roman Catholic parish priest in North Shields, who was the only member living in the North East, and Robert Moore, lecturer in sociology at Aberdeen University.[14] During my twelve years in the job they met with me about twice a year as well as making themselves available for all sorts of 'crisis' occasions. From each of them I learnt an immense amount. John died in 1981, but, although our formal relationship has ceased, I continue to be in contact with David and Robert.

As time went on a matter that increasingly exercised my mind was the question of how the job I was doing might continue in the long term, that is to say after I myself ceased to be engaged as theological consultant. I felt that what I was doing was important and that it would take a long time to effect changes in the overall stance of the church towards the world. It became pretty obvious that few people saw it the way I did, but that in general it was assumed that what I was doing was my own affair and that when I stopped doing it, that would be the end of the matter – and there might be peace in the land! I was not prepared to let matters take this course, so in 1979 I took steps to prepare for a successor and asked a group to review the work that had been done and make recommendations about the future. They produced their report in the same year recommending the continuation of the post. In July 1981 I resigned and in September 1982 the Rev. Dr Peter Sedgwick took up the post now formally constituted as Theological Consultant to the North-East Ecumenical Group.

The theological argument of this book is built around my experiences between 1969 and 1981 when I was employed as Theological Consultant in North-East England. In order to make sense of that period I have said something about my earlier life. (Incidentally I must also point out that my spiritual journey did not end with the ending of my formal employment by the church. I say something about where I *now* am at the end of the book.) Just now I want to sum up the part of my story that I have described so far. I have divided it into two parts: my early experience of God and my time as theological consultant. When I compare the second part of the story with the first I see that there are differences that suggest that I myself have changed and that I have become a very different person. One obvious change is that in my early experience I was overcome by what was happening to *me*, and I felt that I was alone in my experience of God's claim on me and in my search for God. By contrast, in what I say about my life in North-East England there is more about my relationships with others. I now *share* in a journey of faith that is clearly a communal undertaking. It is something we do together in relationships that may be mutually frustrating, but can be mutually supportive. I do not repudiate my early experience. Feelings of abandonment and desolation force us all at some time to recognize that we face the absence or presence of God alone, and that in the end we must take responsibility for what we are and what we do. We cannot hide in the crowd. If we are to penetrate below the superficialities of life, this sense of aloneness is a necessary part of Christian life. What I have learnt is that it is not the only aspect of the Christian journey.

II   What God has Taught Me

What have I learnt from these encounters with God? To believe that God 'speaks' to you is one thing: to know *what* he says is not so clear. When St Francis of Assisi heard God say 'Re-build my church', he immediately set about repairing the derelict building in which he was praying. Only later did he realize that God wanted him to re-build the church's spiritual life. I too at first failed to understand the meaning of my encounters with God. 'You must be a missionary' conjured up for me pictures of distant lands, hot sun and poisonous snakes. (The men in the steel works suffered from the same misapprehension often saying to me 'We don't want missionaries. We're not savages'.) Only later did I discover the missionary needs of this country.

Far from trying to compare myself with a 'Saint' I want to say how 'ordinary' this kind of experience is. At some time or other in the lives of most people I believe God 'speaks' to them. This is not necessarily something dramatic, it may simply be a feeling of disturbance, not being at home with oneself or an undefined longing for something beyond one's grasp or apprehension. How we understand and interpret such promptings depends on our background and culture. We drag up from a subconscious level whatever images we have, whether they are psychological ('the disturbance is due to a disordered mind'), physical ('indigestion'), religious or quasi-religious (God). If we understand the promptings as coming from God, we still have to ask 'What kind of God?' 'What does he want of me?'

For me the discovery of the meaning of God's call did not come in a sudden flash of insight, nor is its meaning yet fully clear, but it is becoming clearer as, in a spirit of prayer and searching, I take small steps of discovery as they open up, beginning from the request to help with the girls' club. This is a journey that is still going on – into the unknown towards a God who cannot be fully known.

It is at the point of experience that theology begins, and it is because the answers to the questions 'What kind of God?' 'What does he want of me?' are not obvious and yet have such profound effect on our lives, that theology is vital. Because people do not agree about what theology is I give my own definition.

Christian theology is that process of reflection by which people come to terms with the meaning of their experience in the light of belief in God as he has revealed himself in Jesus Christ.[1] This involves consideration of their experience in its secular context, consideration of God's revelation of himself in Jesus Christ as this has been understood and lived by throughout Christian history, and the implications this carries for their lives as they respond in their particular circumstances. It is a life long process in which we discover ever new depths in life and in God.

In this chapter I sketch out the theme of this book. As I have already stated, it concerns God and the question 'What kind of God?'. Because our knowledge of God starts from the point when God comes to us in life, theology is woven into the story of actual happenings. In this case I focus on what took place during my time as Theological Consultant in North-East England. I must tell the story in order to make the theology intelligible for that is how theology is done. I must, however, point out that my aim is not to give a domestic account of one piece of the church's work, but to present a theological argument, which is theological precisely because it springs from God's self-revelation in life.

Briefly my argument is this:

First of all it concerns the relation between church/world/ kingdom. Much else depends on getting these basic relationships right. In my own experience nothing could have been plainer than the fact that God made a total demand on my life. This at first filled me with fear, for it meant letting go of all that made me feel secure. Such a sense of God's total demand which is felt by many people, is interpreted in different ways. Some see it as a demand to 'give up the world', so that from that time their lives are lived exclusively in a 'spiritual', 'churchly' world. In this view the church is central and the kingdom has no connection with the present world, I am led to a different conclusion, for in the demand that everything should be brought under God's rule, I now see an invitation to enter the kingdom of God, which potentially includes the whole world. The effect therefore of accepting God's invitation (demand) is not to leave the world, but to see it in a new light. People and events are no longer dull and flat, but have within them the possibilities of God. We are no longer limited to what is finite, but the finite is already reflecting the glory of the infinite. We see things in a three-dimensional way within the eschatological purposes of God. God's power has broken into the world, his kingdom is present now, evil and suffering are being overcome. There are present signs that assure us of the ultimate realization of God's kingdom of love, peace and justice. An eschatological viewpoint gives a further edge to life in that it reminds us that everything is now moving to its end and time is limited. There is the 'now or never' challenge that I felt when I finally gave in to God. We are on the way to, and if we so choose, we may share in the work of the kingdom *now*. In this view the church is secondary in that it is sign and agent of the kingdom.

If the centrality of the kingdom is accepted, we shall attend to the world and listen to what it says for it is in and through the world that God speaks to us.

Many Christians find it difficult to understand that the world itself is data for theological reflection and I often have to justify the fact.

Christians speak of the uniqueness of individuals and of the vocation of each person, but they do not relate this insight to the fact that each person is shaped by their particular situation, and that it is in terms of their situation that they must respond to God. The men I knew in the steel works in Sheffield were *who* they were as a result of their relationship with the industry and the city with all that makes up its life, including the churches. Not only had this history helped to shape them, but they had helped to shape it. The people I worked with in Hong Kong had a different history. Behind them were centuries of Chinese culture that had developed without contact with the Western world, until their colonization by Britain, which though it happened so long ago is still part of their consciousness of *who* they are.

Discovering God in life means discovering him in the life of individuals and communities, and to respond to God requires changes in both. If change is to be effected, the realities of power that affect both individual and community must be reckoned with. This means taking note of the formal and informal structures of society.

God is concerned with *every* aspect of life. He is not to be confined to the 'religious' or 'personal' areas. He calls for the response of individuals in *all* their relationships.

To give value to the world is to give value to people. To see people from the perspective of faith in God is greatly to expand our expectations of people. Created in the image of God there is no limit to what people can be. I grieve when I see human beings put upon by society and ignored by the church so that the struggling flame of God's spirit in them is quenched. We should be working with God against all that oppresses humanity – for a more human world.

But 'humanism' is an epithet of abuse in a church that, being centred on itself, is dismissive of all that is not church and does not see the possibilities of people. Putting the 'spiritual' in opposition to the 'human' it turns to people and to the world a face that is cold and inhuman.

This brings me to the heart of what I have learnt and am learning about God – his love for humanity. Our own experience of the limitations of love and the lovelessness of life contradicts the notion of God as love. The church in its projection of a God who looks down on the world and demands a high moral standard, leads people to despair of themselves. We are only too aware that we are unlovable, yet we still long for love.

Jesus Christ reveals God's affirmation of our humanity and how the love of God can be a reality in a loveless world. In the face of the opposition of hatred and wrong, crucifixion is inevitable. It does not make sense of our suffering but it assures us that God is in it with us. In the evils and sufferings of the world only a God who suffers with us is recognizable as a God of love.

Why have a church if world and kingdom are God's primary concern? So some people argue. But, rather than doing away with the need for church, this perspective helps us to see the true calling of the church to be servant of the kingdom in the world.

This requires the church to exist in two forms:

> as gathered church in which Jesus is present in the teaching, fellowship, breaking of bread and prayers, and
> as dispersed church, which in the world encounters Jesus in the hungry, naked, sick and imprisoned.

In the church's gathered form the memory of Jesus is treasured and reflected upon. In its dispersed form all that is happening in the world is interpreted in the light of that memory.

Both forms are essential to the church's ability to fulfil its task. But the church today recognizes only one form, the gathered church, as norm. It thereby fails to enable discipleship in the world, fails the world and in consequence is unsatisfactory even to itself. Two aspects of the church, which properly belong together have been severed, so that those who venture to serve the world feel unsupported by the community of belief. An inevitable result is that for those who serve, questions are raised about the relevance not only of the church, but of God.

The kind of church we have depends on the kind of God we have. If God loves the world, the church too must be open to the world. It must hear in the sufferings of the world the questions the world asks about itself and about God: 'What hope is there for the world?' 'Can there be a God of love when the world is like this?'

Many Christians are concerned about the godlessness of the world. But to believe in God still leaves open the question 'What kind of God?' The Jews to whom Jesus came were a deeply religious people with a strong belief in God, and it was in their religiousness that Jesus posed to them the question of God, and it was this that led to conflict and crucifixion. Today the church should be posing the question 'What kind of God?' to the world.

Instead of the church questioning the world's assumptions about itself and posing to it the question of God, it is the world that today questions the church about the authenticity of the God it proclaims. A remote, all powerful, impassive God cannot answer the world's needs. A soft, indulgent God who takes no account of injustice will not suffice. Only a God who suffers in the sufferings of humanity can save. That is the God I meet in the world, find with me in whatever knocks I myself take, and recognize in Jesus Christ and in the memory of Jesus Christ. The church should be like its God. In what it is and does as well as in what it says, it should answer the world's questions and show the authenticity of God as love.

But in so many ways the church is unlike the God revealed in Jesus Christ:

Instead of seeing God's glory in ordinary people and everyday things, it separates itself from what is 'material' and 'human' and preaches a 'spiritual' gospel.

Instead of being concerned about the divisions between people, giving special consideration as Jesus did to the poor and the outcast, it finds it hard to make contact with the poor and its membership is mainly from the respectable better-off classes.

Instead of opposing injustice and wrong in the world, it is afraid to be involved in conflict.

Instead of relating its tradition to present experience in order to discover God's word to today's world, it assumes it already possesses complete knowledge of God.

Instead of organizing itself systematically for its task in the world, making use of the best management skills available in the community, it is ponderously concerned with its own business and acts only spasmodically in the world as a result of outside pressures.

Instead of enabling people to share in a communal journey contributing freely to the cause of the kingdom, it inhibits people, keeping them in a state of dependency, like a flock of sheep!

No wonder the world finds no answer to its questions. No wonder people do not look to the church in their need. No wonder the majority of people are totally estranged and separated from a church whose God has no earthly connection with their lives.

The reason for this contradiction of its faith is that the church has lost its vision of *who* God is.

My experience convinced me that until the church faces up to fundamental matters of belief it is stuck. It was this conviction that led me to accept the job of theological consultant and to make what I did of this open brief. I saw that if we were to get faith, belief and action moving we must get theology going. Ways must be opened up by which people everywhere could share in the exploration of those matters that touched their lives in the light of Christian faith, so that they might find grace and wisdom by which to live.

Whereas the church in its present practice starts its theology from the Bible and Christian tradition I was convinced that our search for God should start with our experience of life. It was on the basis of this belief that I formed my understanding of what it was to be a theological consultant.

If people are to discover God as he is *now*, they need to reflect on their present experience in the light of the Christian tradition. In this enterprise the help people need is not that of a 'theological *teacher*' who gives information about Christian beliefs, though certain information is needed. It is that of a 'theological *consultant*,' who will help them to discover the meaning of those beliefs in their lives. This means digging deeply into their experience in order to discover God *in* it as well as digging deeply into Christian tradition in order to recognize God in our experiences. A 'theological *teacher*' tends to tell people what to think and what to believe. A 'theological *consultant*' helps people to think for themselves and, in the light of Christian tradition, to make their own discovery of God.

Professional theologians are not the only people who have knowledge of God. Every Christian has some knowledge of God, and many people, who would not call themselves Christians, have experience of God even though they may not recognize it as such.

In the North-East Region as in any other place I believe there are many potential and actual theological skills. The need is to release, develop and put them to work appropriately. This will not happen unless people are given more help. 'Help' in this context means providing frameworks in which people can clarify their questions and tackle them systematically, and opening up the resources of Christian tradition. The theological consultant's job is not to spread her/his own theological outlook, but to work with others so that they may develop and articulate *their* theological understandings.

My aim was, and is, to encourage all sorts of people to join with me and with others on a journey and search for God. This does not consist in a steady progress towards an ever clearer picture of God, but is a journey deeper into the mystery of God.

As we journey we form our own images of where we are going and of God. Because it is impossible to form a complete picture of God these images are necessarily inadequate, but some are more helpful than others. One thing that struck me forcibly during my time as theological consultant was that Christians were operating on different models of what Christian faith is about and that this had extremely negative effects. It is this theme of conflicting patterns of belief that I develop in the next chapter.

III   Conflicting Patterns of Belief

When one comes up against a disagreement among Christians it is not always helpful to focus on the particular matter in question. In order to understand each other it is often necessary to look at our total patterns or, as I prefer to say, models of belief. In my experience I have found a comparison of models a helpful way forward and I therefore spend some time in this chapter on the subject. A model is a way of putting together a number of different factors in order to see how they relate to each other. To give a crude example: If God is seen primarily as a judge and the end of the world as a separation of the good people from the bad, a whole view of life follows. If on the other hand God is seen as an indulgent Father Christmas people behave in a quite different way. Scientists construct models to see how different elements react upon each other. In doing this they sometimes make diagrams, for instance of the structure of the atom. The atom does not *look* like this, but the diagram/model enables scientists to capture their thinking about the relationships and energies of the atom and on that basis to make practical experiments as a result of which the model may well be revised. Christians need to think through their total models and so to gain some idea about how the various doctrines of Christian faith belong together rather than seeing them as separate items.

Two things need to be emphasized. First, in using models scientists are concerned with how change occurs. Christian faith is also about change, and a Christian use of models can help in replacing what is too often a static with a dynamic understanding of faith and its effects. Secondly, models help us to see things in their various relationships. The matter of relationship is crucial, for our understanding of God affects our understanding of everything else, and our understanding of everything else affects our understanding of God. God can only be understood in his relationships with the world and with humanity. If, for instance we have a low view of our fellow human beings, this relates in some way to our view of God. If God seems irrelevant to our day to day life that impinges on our attitude to life. We need comprehensive models that show how a lot of different things fit together.

There are different perspectives on Christian faith, upon which different people operate. If we are to understand each other and work together (though not necessarily to agree on everything), we need to examine our different models. Models do not necessarily have to be set out in a diagrammatic form, but in practice I have found a visual method helpful. To set beliefs down in such a form is of course a very rough and ready approach. The aim is to help us to talk to each other about beliefs which neither words nor diagrams can fully express. The diagrams are only starting points for discussion, but they are at least starting points.

If we think again of the scientists' use of models we note that there is no question of a model being right or wrong. It is either helpful or unhelpful in clarifying the dynamics of a process so that the scientist can go on to take the next step in his thinking. The same is true of theological models. No model is absolutely right, but it may help us forward in our thinking. A model must be tested against the actual experience of life. When it is found that the facts do not fit the model, we should not force them to fit our model, but should change, adapt or scrap the model and construct a new one. Many Christians do not act in this way, but try to *force* all experiences into their particular model of belief.[1]

In the course of describing my activities as theological consultant I shall continually refer to problems and blockages concerning the practice of Christian discipleship and ministry. I do not believe that these difficulties can be overcome by dealing with each one on its own, for the difficulties often relate to the fact that people are trying to respond to their situation out of inappropriate models of Christian faith.

The two models in Diagram 1[2] illustrate the nature of the problem. The comparison between them is inevitably crude, for no one fits neatly into any one model. We are all a bit mixed up. Together we are engaged in a search for truth, in the process of which we shall continually have to construct new models.

The first model (a) emphasizes God's redemptive activity through the historical Jesus who atoned for our sins. It depicts those who do not overtly confess Jesus as Lord and Saviour as being without hope because they are outside his saving grace. It contrasts the old and the new creations; they are mutually

Diagram 1

(a) Salvation Model

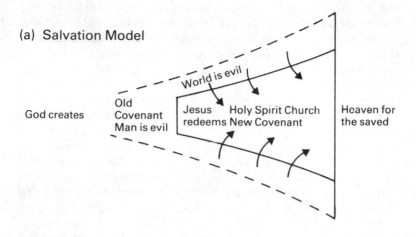

God creates

Old
Covenant
Man is evil

World is evil

Jesus   Holy Spirit Church
redeems   New Covenant

Heaven for
the saved

(b) Creation Model

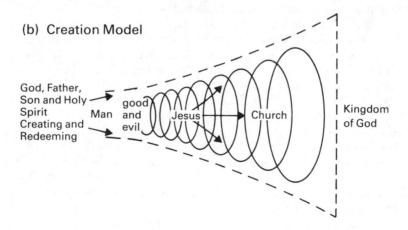

God, Father,
Son and Holy
Spirit
Creating and
Redeeming

Man

good
and
evil

Jesus

Church

Kingdom
of God

exclusive, the first is predominantly evil and the other good. It divides the 'saved' from the 'unsaved'. It emphasizes what God contributes – and what he alone can contribute to man's salvation, and denigrates man's own part in his salvation and growth. . . . It contrasts the goodness of God with the sinfulness of man and the holiness of the saved with the evilness of the unsaved. It depicts God's primary activity as saving and redeeming evil man from an evil world to find salvation in Christ and new and eternal life in his new creation and in the church. It is a model about a sick world in need of saving, healing and redeeming.

The second model (b) emphasizes God as the creator. It depicts him – and Jesus the second person of the Trinity and the Holy Spirit – as actively engaged from first to last in every aspect of the created order. It depicts him as effecting a new creation through the redeeming activity of Jesus in the church and in the world. It depicts a process of human creative activity both within the church and within the world which is an inextricable mixture of good and bad. It shows that powerful thrusts towards goodness and betterment spring from the depths of human beings of every kind and of every age as well as thrusts towards evil and change for the worse; viz. within humanity there are constructive as well as destructive tendencies. It depicts creation as a process within which God and man can co-operate but which God started and which he will end and fulfil.[3]

A further contrast is between the way in which the two models see the relationship between church and kingdom. This is such a fundamental divide that it needs a word of explanation. Though it is agreed that the kingdom of God is central to Jesus' message, there is disagreement among Christians about what the kingdom is.

For some it is a totally future hope for the individual. 'Heaven' is promised to the faithful *after* death. Life is a preparation for the kingdom and the material world is only a backcloth for human endeavour, with no lasting significance of its own.

An opposite view is that Jesus inaugurated the kingdom in *this* world and that there are present signs of its reality. God's end purpose is that the kingdom of the world shall become 'the Kingdom of our Lord and of his Christ' (Rev. 11.15), and that all things shall be united in Christ 'things in heaven and things on earth' (Eph. 1.10). This is the end towards which things are moving *now*. Many people contribute to this purpose without knowing that they do so. Christians, because they know what this purpose is, contribute consciously to God's purpose. This is not a purely individual hope but hope for the world and for all humanity.

These conflicting views lead to different understandings of the relation of church and kingdom and affect every aspect of Christian belief.

In model (a) the church is centre stage (see Diagram 2(a)) evil man is redeemed from an evil world to find salvation in Christ and in the church. 'There is no salvation outside the church.' God's activity through the Holy Spirit is confined to the church. If God is to reach the world this must happen through the church and if the world is to reach God this can only happen through the church. The church *goes out* with a known gospel to be *applied* to the world. In this view the kingdom of God is 'heaven' – a different state of existence into which the 'saved' enter when they die. Finally the present world will come to an end, nothing in it and nothing done in it has any lasting significance. Then the full number of the saved will enter into a state of bliss in heaven.

In model (b) the kingdom is central. The kingdom is the focus of God's activity, and God's purpose is the realization of his rule throughout the whole universe and through all humanity. God's Spirit is at work in the world as well as in the church and in all people, whether they acknowledge him or not (see Diagram 2(b)). The kingdom in all its fullness will be the gift of God and it is towards its completion that God is moving all things. The kingdom is present now and, though there is no steady progress towards its completion, there are ephemeral signs of its presence. Though the final kingdom is an eschatological event, there are links between this world and the next as there were between the earthly and the risen body of Jesus. His resurrection is a sign and a promise of the final recreation of *all* things.

The church in this perspective is not in the centre of the stage, but it has a specific and vital place in the creative/redemption process. It has no ready-made gospel to apply *to* the world, but has to discover God *in* the world. There it must point to 'signs' and work with God to produce further signs of the presence of the kingdom. Its task is to be a sign itself by demonstrating the nature of the kingdom in its own life, and to be an agent of the kingdom by working to transform the world, so that it approximates more nearly to the kingdom. It may appear in this model that the distinction between world and church has been blurred for it shows that not only is God present to all people, but that

Diagram 2

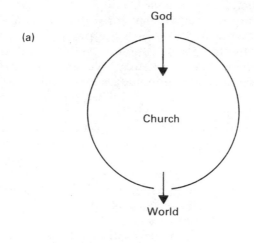

(a)

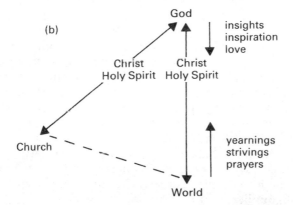

(b)

people of all sorts turn to him in yearnings strivings and prayers even though they do not know or acknowledge him. There is however a vital difference and that is that the church consists of those who *know* who God is. Its task therefore includes interpreting to the world the meaning of its yearnings, strivings and prayers and helping people to *know* the God whom they have already met but have not recognized.

These models are useful in that they help us to identify two different approaches to Christian faith that are commonly held, and they can help us begin to talk across this divide. They have, however, considerable weaknesses.

Both models are two rather than three dimensional and are unable to convey the way in which the present is permeated eschatologically by the final salvation of God. The information they do give is, moreover, too sketchy. We need to know more: Model (a) shows that we are under judgment and that we need to be saved, but it does not suggest *from* what, *for* what or *by* what kind of God we may be saved. Model (b) affirms God's active presence in the world, but it does not help us to understand the nature of his power, the obstacles encountered, or how we may share in his purposes.

A more serious weakness is that this kind of polarization leads to the exclusion of essential aspects of Christian faith. They present us with a choice between salvation *or* creation, kingdom *or* church, whereas *all* these factors are vital.

Because neither of these models is satisfactory, we need a third model that includes the positive points of both models and sets them in an eschatological perspective indicating the dynamic tension between present and future, reality and promise, this world and that which transcends it, humanity and God.

One way to envisage this eschatological tension is to super-impose one model upon the other. In diagrammatic form this might look pretty chaotic, but the point is that a lot of things are going on at once, and there is a powerful dynamic in life, which biblically is seen as 'crisis'. In this situation choices have to be made and action taken NOW.

The attempt to get a helpful model is not a hair-splitting exercise but a matter of vital practical concern. Our understanding of the kind of process we are involved in, determines what we actually *do* with our lives.

In Diagram 3 a sketch of a third model (c) represents my own view of the process.

I start from model (b) in which Father, Son and Holy Spirit are from the beginning active throughout the world continuously creating and redeeming. In this model the kingdom of God is a key motif and redemption is not simply of individuals but of the whole world.

In contrast with model (b) however, I emphasize the significance of Jesus, and because he has meaning for the whole process, I do not follow model (a) in making a hard line between the old and new covenants. Jesus of Nazareth reveals a process that has

Diagram 3

(c)

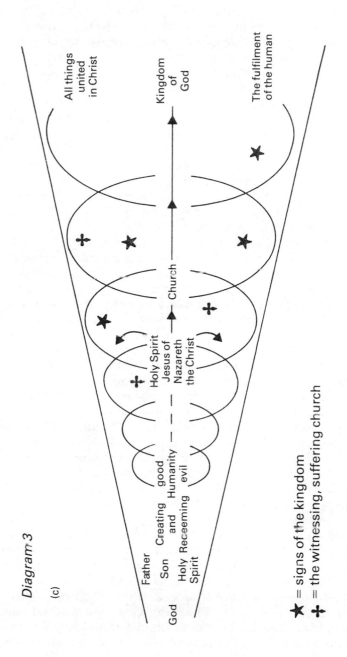

All things
united
in Christ

Kingdom
of
God

The fulfilment
of the human

Father

Son

Holy
Spirit

God

Creating   good
and
Humanity — — —
Redeeming   evil

Holy Spirit
Jesus of
Nazareth
the Christ

Church

★ = signs of the kingdom

✛ = the witnessing, suffering church

been going on all the time, for he reveals God as he always is in his nature of seeking and saving love. Jesus is the clue that enables us to make sense of the past, present and future of a world that otherwise makes no sense.

But Jesus is not just the bearer of information. In Jesus' announcement 'The kingdom of God is at hand', events take a new turn for God actually begins to govern and therefore to manifest himself as God in the world of men. God's kingdom is the divine power itself in its saving activity within our history, and at the same time it is the 'final, eschatological state of affairs that brings to an end a world that is dominated by the forces of calamity and woe, and initiates a new world'.[4] There is a here and now dynamic of God's exercise of control *and* the definitive state of good to which God's saving activity is directed. Thus present and future are essentially interrelated.

Today many Christians have a passive attitude in relation to the world as if all that is needed is to wait for the end. This contradicts the explosiveness of the New Testament. In order to express the extraordinary effect Jesus had on them, the first Christians used the interpretative tools that were available, and it is the eschatological framework that gives the dynamic edge to their story.

There were in Jesus' time a number of variations on the eschatological theme, in many of which hopes of salvation were seen in terms of God's coming intervention in judgment on the world, for the salvation of his people and with an outpouring of his spirit on all flesh. Without going into details, the point to be made is that the first Christians identified Jesus with the one who was to be specially anointed with God's Spirit, that is to say the Christ, to be instrumental in bringing in God's kingdom.

The Christians did not take over current ideas wholesale, but developed them on the basis of the actual facts of Jesus. Among the facts with which they had to come to terms, was Jesus' rejection and crucifixion. One way in which they made sense of this astonishing fact was by seeing in Jesus' suffering the beginnings of the woes that were expected to herald the end of the old and the start of the new era. Because they believed that in Jesus the new era had already begun they felt the extreme urgency of their situation. The kingdom *is* already here, the process *is* moving towards an end, there is no cause for despair and every reason to press forward. God's will *will* be done, evil *can* be overcome, love *is* stronger than hatred. *God looks to men and women to make his rule operational in the world* – and there is not all the time in the world. Come on you Christians, 'lift your drooping hands and strengthen your weak knees' (Heb. 12.12). We have to oppose with all our might everything in the world that is contrary to God's kingdom of justice, love and peace. This has to be done by following in the way of Jesus.

In model (b) the person of Jesus is only vaguely noted, and this indicates the embarrassment with which today many people consider that figure. There is a proper reaction against weak and sentimental images of Jesus. Many of the repeated calls to accept 'Jesus as your personal Saviour' omit the thought of 'Jesus as Saviour of the world'. I have said that my third model highlights the centrality of Jesus but I want to go beyond current limited and limiting pictures of Jesus. In order to do this we must look again at the Gospels.

The eschatological framework of the New Testament enables us to see Jesus not as an isolated figure, but in his relation to God and to the working out of God's purposes in the world. Jesus reveals a mystery which is not new, but which until his coming in the flesh had remained hidden (Eph. 3.4).

In my model (c) Jesus the Christ is seen within a Trinitarian understanding of God. There is no final break between the old and new covenants but a line runs back from the historical Jesus of Nazareth to the beginning of creation. The line also runs forward to show Jesus present in the Spirit in the world and throughout history. He is also ahead of us where in the fulfilment of the kingdom of God he will appear in glory.

The focal point for our understanding of God's processes in the world is the historical life of Jesus of Nazareth. In this human life we are firmly brought down to earth. Jesus of Nazareth revealed the truth about God and the truth about humanity. He challenged and continues to challenge all preconceived notions of God, all sentimental and stylized pictures of the Christ *and* all utopian or cynical views of human beings. What should be clear on any reading of the New Testament is that Jesus exercised an immense attraction upon people, and that to be in his presence and to share table fellowship with him was to experience fulfilment, joy and salvation.

Jesus' conviviality and message of good news was often contrasted with John the Baptist's asceticism and message of judgment. In Jesus God says 'no' to all the misery of life. God seeks the well-being of people, without laying down conditions. God gives himself totally for the sake of mankind and the cause of

God is the cause of mankind. The church often displays a low view of man. In the person of Jesus we see what persons essentially are and what they can be. 'We are God's children now; it does not yet appear what we shall be, but we know that when he appears we shall be like him, for we shall see him as he is' (I John 3.2).

Meanwhile we get glimpses of Jesus in our fellow human beings, and in them we meet God. In line with this insight a striking feature of Jesus' life is his acceptance of people as they are and the fact that he goes out of his way to meet and mix with outcasts. Only the personal impact of Jesus can account for the continuation of the movement that started with him and the creation and persistence of the church that is commissioned to carry his movement forward. The end of the process, the fulfilment of the kingdom of God is also the fulfilment of the *humanum* – that is humanity complete and at one.

In my third model (c) as well as bringing into relief the person of Jesus I also sharpen and clarify the place of the church. The image of the church as a box in model (a) totally misrepresents what the church is meant to be. What Jesus condemned most of all in the religious groups of his day from Pharisees to Zealots, was their exclusiveness and sectarianism. What shocked these groups most in Jesus' behaviour was the fact that he did not limit God's concern to those who were 'worthy', but went out of his way to mix with 'sinners'. In my diagram (model (c)) I show the church as a simple line, open and exposed to the world, yet having an identity of its own that is represented by the line that links it to Jesus of Nazareth and continues forward following Jesus' way to God and the kingdom of God.

It is Jesus who gives the church its identity, but (although I cannot show this in the diagram) I must stress that in contrast with any 'Jesus and me' individualism, or claustrophobic matey-ness the church is a *communion* of persons.

The New Testament accounts of the resurrection appearance of Jesus show that the church sprang, not from the gathering together of a number of converted individuals, but from *communal* experiences of Jesus' living presence after his death, from *communal* experiences of forgiveness and from a *communal* mission charge to continue to proclaim the good news of the kingdom of God.

I depict the church in two ways. First as gathered church represented by a line from Jesus that moves forward witnessing by its life and its proclamation to Jesus. Secondly as the church dispersed seeking the signs of the kingdom in the world (shown as stars in the diagram), seeking those who are lost and getting involved in the misery of the world. This latter aspect of the church's life is represented by crosses that indicate the historical sufferings of Christians as they follow the way of Jesus Christ in opposing all that is contrary to God's kingdom. These two different representations together indicate the same church, the one body of Christ. Insofar as the church follows the way of Jesus Christ it has an essential place in God's purposes.

The problem of portraying my meaning in diagrammatic form is that I wish to depict everything in three dimensional terms. The eschatological view that I have tried to describe points to an overlapping of the ages. In one sense we *now* live in the kingdom of God. God is present to save *now*. The church is not simply a human institution but an eschatological fellowship within which we *already* experience the joy of table fellowship with Christ and his saints. The glory of God which will be revealed in all its fullness at the end, already penetrates the world and human life. This belief should not lull us into a passive feeling of security, but should spur us to risk ourselves in the service of the world, which is the service of God and his kingdom.

In this chapter I have spoken of the need for each of us to have a model by which we can see the overall dynamic of our faith. In subsequent chapters I put more detail on some aspects of my own model (c), but here I must leave it as an impressionistic sketch.

I have spent some time on models, for I have found that the use of models, however crude they may be, has helped me to see more deeply into the practical mission problems and possibilities of the church.

When, for instance, I find clergy recoiling from the problems of the city (see Chapter V) I realize that this is not simply a matter of lack of time, but the lack of a positive attitude towards the world, and of the belief that God comes to meet them from within the world.

When I hear Christians saying that they will share in a Lent course on evangelism, but not in one on unemployment, I know that it is our different understandings of the whole movement of God's purposes in the world that have to be explored.

When someone says 'I cannot believe in God when so many people are suffering', I know that their total world view needs to be examined.

We cannot talk about God in the abstract but must understand him in his relationships with people and with the world. I conclude that in the day to day differences among church people, about quite practical matters of mission and maintenance, what is ultimately at stake is our understanding of God.

Before concluding this discussion of models I want to point out that in the same way that our beliefs relate to each other in patterns, so that we cannot discuss differences concerning one particular doctrine without taking note of how it fits into an overall perspective or model, so our activities form specific patterns.

In my work as theological consultant, I could not hope to change patterns of belief by one single approach. Systems of belief are built up by many inter-related factors and change can only take place by a multi-form approach, the exact nature of which will be shaped by the possibilities of the situation.

I well remember how the full force of what this implies bore in on me during the first discussion of the advisory group. I had thought that I had a fairly broad concept of what my job should be, but this seemed extremely limited in the light of the possibilities outlined by the group. John with the support of Robert, pointed out that if I were to provide a *context* of theological thinking I needed to take account of *all* aspects of life in the region. Before long I had a huge length of wall paper on the floor and was marking it out in columns.

The chart we produced looked formidable. In fact it was only one way of focussing the main questions which I should bear in mind:

1. What are the main issues for people in this region?
2. What insights on these issues can be gained from sociology?
3. What are the churches' (ecumenically) main activities? What gospel insights are they bringing into play?
4. What gospel insights appear to be relevant to the issues of the region? ((1) above). What are the main Christian doctrines, which though they do not obviously appear to be relevant, need to be kept before us?

The purpose was that I should, in my various activities and explorations, observe and listen so that I could note on the chart whatever struck me as being important, and my reflections on it. The framework was purely for my own use as a background to help me not to get stuck in one part of life, and to discover over a period of time the interconnections between the different areas of life. I mention this, because though, with my advisory group, I worked out a strategy for the job and was quite persistent in following it through, few people realized that there was any pattern in my activities. Each person saw only the part of the work that he or she was involved in, and even senior clergy, who should have known better, described me as 'working with a number of groups', as if that summed up the total meaning of my job.

The truth was that each of my engagements – industrial mission, urban ministry, lay training and so on, were different ways of tackling the same aim – to clarify and deepen an understanding of discipleship and of God.

In the discussions of the advisory group a complete pattern did not emerge at once. It was a matter of taking one step at a time and then deciding, in the light of what happened, what the next step should be. One point upon which we all agreed, on which my mind has not changed, and which from our first meeting set us on a different course from most of the church, was that theological reflection should start from life.

IV God and World

I spent my first Sunday in the North East with young men from one of the large firms and listened to them talking about their first impressions of entering the world of work. These young men were being powerfully shaped by work, technology, large institutions, secular views of the world, specific values, patterns of authority, images of their own worth and that of other people. *Who* they are as individuals is inseparable from the society of which they are a part. It is within all these relationships and pressures that people are looking for identity, vision, hope, humanity and purpose. But people do not imagine that God has much to do with the modern world, and neither the church nor its God is seen as a resource.

In this chapter I ask 'How can people discover God in our world?' I relate my discussion to my experience with the two Industrial Missions in the North East, the Northumbrian Industrial Mission and the Teesside Industrial Mission.

Technology is the dominant feature of our society.[1] It affects everything – communications, medicine, leisure, home, how we live, how we think and the way our society is organized. Today fewer people work in manufacturing industry, and the church, which was never able to come to terms with industry, turns back with relief to its traditional concern with home and leisure. But this will not do. Production (including agricultural production), commerce, distribution, the economy, remain at the centre of life and of political concern. Today's culture and today's social relationships, with all their class and sex demarcations, have been shaped by industry. Massive unemployment and struggles by workers to retain their jobs in industries such as mining, take place not in the past but today.

In the past, life for most people most of the time appeared to be subject to inexplicable and uncontrollable forces, the operation of which were attributed to an all powerful God. Today it is science and technology that seem to be in control. Though they cannot yet control all things or answer all our questions, they have changed our whole view of life and in doing so have put in question previous ways of understanding God. Today it is clear that:

> people have real power and responsibility in the world, but Christianity says that God is Almighty and people are worthless and weak:
> the things that most concern people are to do with work, housing and living standards, but Christianity takes a negative view of the material world:
> life is governed by institutions and change requires co-operation, but Christianity preaches individual salvation:
> science and technology create ever new futures, but Christianity is resistant to change:
> new responses are needed in a new situation, but Christianity preaches a timeless gospel.

These contradictions re-enforce the notion that God has little to do with the world. How can people be helped to see that this is not the case?

Industrial mission is one of the ways in which the church is tackling the question of God's relationship with the world and what this means for Christian faith and mission.

My first contact with industrial mission was in the early days of the Sheffield Industrial Mission. It is fashionable in industrial mission circles today to decry this early work as being 'dated'. It is however worth looking back to the inspiration behind a movement that has such potential significance for the mission of the church.

The origin of today's movement lies largely in the Sheffield Industrial Mission, which with the appointment of 'Ted' Wickham as its first chaplain was started in 1944 by Leslie Hunter (Bishop of Sheffield 1939–62).

In a Diocesan letter entitled 'Evangelism' Bishop Hunter expressed reasons which led him later to set up the industrial mission. His first concern was with *evangelism*:

> In industrial society a new phenomenon as far as we know has arisen – namely, multitudes who are neither bad nor worldly . . . but are apparently without any feeling of spiritual need. They are mass-producing and mass-produced. . . .

These immense populations are the unresisting product of a machine age, and it is going to be uncommonly hard to get through to any thought or aspiration which might become a hunger for God.

Evangelism required first of all a robust *theology*:

> All the missions and revivals which have had staying power and have borne much fruit have had a core of belief – an intellectual backbone – yes, theology. . . . In recent times, a lack of intellectual robustness and an excess of sentimental-ism . . . have contributed to the loss of a virile faith amongst the people in the living God of Christ's revealing.

Secondly it demanded a *prophetic concern with the world*:

> The new evangelism must be more than a speaking war. . . . It will direct its energy both against the hindrances to the good life in the social order and against outmoded machinery and all uncharitableness in the churches. . . .
> Every member of the Church must have it burnt into his mind that the Church is set in the world to redeem it.

Thirdly, while taking the church as his starting place, Bishop Hunter was severely critical of the church in its current form:

> The Church must never for a moment be a pious clique keeping itself to itself, but a saving, serving, apostolic society.[2]

These statements show that the inspiration behind industrial mission was both evangelistic and prophetic.

When I joined the staff of the Sheffield Industrial Mission in 1959 my aim was primarily evangelistic for I wanted to help people who were outside the influence of the church to come to a living faith. I was however well aware that this could only be done within a concern for people in the whole context of their lives.

In 1969 when on my return from Hong Kong I again came into contact with industrial mission in Britain, I found considerable changes of emphasis in the two industrial missions with which I worked and throughout the country. Evangelism was now seen not as related to but as opposed to prophecy. A controversy within industrial mission divided those who maintained a practice of regular factory visiting from those whose work was 'issue centred'. The first were disparaged as taking the 'easy option' of pastoral personal work as against the 'prophetic' stance of the second.

Obviously any movement that does not change soon becomes moribund, what we have to consider is the cause of the changes and how these relate to past and present aims of industrial mission. Are these changes due to normal processes of growing or do they indicate theological confusions? What indications do they give of the health of industrial mission and its potential for the future?

The first reason for change is the reality of the situation. It is easy to prescribe theoretical aims, but it is not so easy to put them into practice. Chaplains rightly speak of 'learning from industry', and there is much that church people, including many who work there, need to learn about industry. Economic, political and industrial powers impress upon people a whole view of life that contradicts that which is presented by the churches (see the first pages of this chapter). Our individualism needs to be replaced by a corporate and more inclusive understanding of Christian faith. People need to see the whole of life, including the world economic powers, in the light of faith in God. Christianity has to make sense of, that is to say it has to change, the situation as well as changing individuals. Personal evangelism that pulls people *out* of their situation has a perverting rather than a converting effect. An 'ark' theology needs to be replaced by a 'kingdom' theology (Chapter III models (a) and (b)). In kingdom theology to tackle particular industrial issues is a necessary approach.

Since the early days of industrial mission the situation has got harder. At the end of World War II there was a sense of hope in the possibility of making a better world, and there was some agreement among people in approaching the task. Today optimism and consensus have given way to cynicism, division and a sharpening of the issues.

There have also been changes in the church. The church today is numerically weaker than it was in the 1940s and 50s. Different responses have been made to this change. In some cases these have consisted in turning inwards in an attempt to strengthen the interior life of the church. In others it has been a matter of turning outwards to adapt theology to a changing world. These opposite tendencies are to some extent represented in the models (a) and (b) described in the last chapter. Whereas most of the churches followed model (a), industrial mission in its concern for the world has followed the creation model (b).

By recovering the fundamental truth that God's purposes concern the transformation of all things, industrial mission has freed itself from the restrictions of a faith that is dominated by the theme of individual salvation (a). It sets the search for faith in a wider context and so makes it potentially more widely accessible. Far from seeing the world as totally evil it stresses the fact that the world is God's creation and that it is good. Man should not be seen primarily as sinner, but as being in the image of God, not helplessly dependent on God but co-creator with God. God has given him abilities to use in the development of nature for the good of people. In contrast with the many Christians who are extremely negative about technology, industrial mission sees God's hand in technology:

> Christian faith, Biblical faith, affirms the 'Providential' character of the creation and the call of man, through science, technology and industry, to utilize the potentials of creation 'for the glory of God and the relief of man's estate'.[3]

In contrast with the individualism of model (a) industrial mission points to the communal implications of God's call, the significance of institutions and the fact that God's purpose concerns the salvation of the whole world. The mission's activities do not centre on personal pastoral work, but on the issues of industry. In the North East for instance it has grappled with questions of participation in industry, responses to rapid social change, the handling of redundancies and plant closures, and massive unemployment.

By this concern with social and industrial issues industrial mission claims to be exercising a 'prophetic' ministry. But is there more to prophecy than simply being socially concerned? Is industrial mission justified in saying that it exercises a 'prophetic' ministry? It is the validity of this claim that we must now examine.

Prophecy in the Bible concerns insights that are given by God into the reality of God and his purposes for the world. Prophecy is true or false according to whether it does or does not relate to reality – that is to God's reality. The question must be asked 'How far is industrial mission's social concern being consciously related to God and the purposes of God?' 'Do the insights that industrial mission offers go beyond those which might come from any thoughtful and informed person or is there a new slant that comes from a perspective of faith in the God of Christ's revealing?'

The Old Testament prophets were clear that God is involved in history and they were concerned with the nation as a whole and with the social issues of their time. In the face of mistaken ideas about God, they presented people with a God of righteousness and justice, who demanded the same of his people.

Many people today claim to speak about the issues of our time in the name of God. Without really understanding what is happening they pronounce blanket condemnations of our society as 'materialistic, permissive etc.'. This externalizing of the problem is not prophecy. The strength of industrial mission is that it speaks from within a situation which it patiently tries to understand from the different points of view of those involved in it.

Over the years industrial mission has worked hard to understand what is happening from the *inside*, and by working alongside people, in employment and unemployment, has helped them to try out new practices and discover unused talents. In this way the fatalism that is the norm in relation to most current issues is denied and as people discover that things do not always have to remain the same, there is a renewal of hope.

Though industrial mission may say little about God, its concern with issues of social justice has more effect than any number of words on changing people's images of God.

But – simply to be socially concerned is not to be prophetic, and simply to say that the world is good is to turn a blind eye to the destructive aspects of technology and industry:

> For many people 'industry' means strikes, disruption of services, violence on the picket lines. It still means factory chimneys and dirt, unemployment and inequality, mass production and shift work, profitability at all costs, a cuckoo which offers goodies to a community, makes them dependent on it, takes what it wants, and then disappears with the proceeds. For many people 'industry' means the combination of interests which holds the power to destroy the only way of life they know.[4]

In the 1960s industrial mission's positive view of the world tended to be an uncritical acceptance of the world and, in the matter of critical judgment on the world, industrial mission still falls short of prophecy. Prophecy in the Old Testament confronts people with the truth of their situation as it is seen from the perspective of faith in a God of righteousness. The prophets held out hope, but it was hope based on a realistic assessment of, and response to the situation. Without judgment, without change of direction, there was no hope: '*If* you are willing and obedient, you shall eat the good of the land: But *if* you refuse and rebel, you shall be devoured by the sword' (Isa. 1.19, 20).

My experience of industrial mission is that, though it may identify some of the key issues in society, it finds it difficult to get beyond the stage of analysis. In meeting after meeting the chart paper goes up on the wall and before long a list of questions or issues appears on it. Having drawn up a list of issues people find it difficult to know what to do with them, and there the process stops.

Prophecy discerns in the light of the reality of God, 'the signs of the times', that is the key issue in a situation, and on this basis points to choices that have to be made in the light of God's judgment on the situation and on the individuals and groups concerned. It holds out hope that is conditional on judgment, choice and response.

It is always difficult for people to face what is wrong in themselves and in their group. This is made more problematic by the fact that people expect the church to condemn and to do this on the most trivial grounds. One man for instance said to me: 'I am disqualified from the start, because I drink.'

What is needed is a recovery of a *radical* understanding of sin, that is to say an understanding of sin that is not apoplectic about secondary matters, but that gets down to the root causes of what is destroying people in our society. Sin has become part of the assumptions and organization of our society, so that its negative aspects cannot be laid at the door of any one individual. Rather than personalizing the issue we need to examine what is meant by 'sin in the structures'.

Sin is that which deliberately contradicts the values of God's kingdom and the character of God as righteousness, justice, freedom and love. Sin, instead of enhancing life, destroys life. It is deadly and we need to be saved from it and from its effects. Sin is built into our structures so that many people in large organizations feel that they do not count, children leave school with a sense of failure, the most needy people get least from the social services, nations in which most people want to live at peace, go to war, and the arms trade becomes the biggest money spinner in British industry.

None of these things are caused by the decisions and choices of single individuals, nor can they be changed by individuals acting alone. They are caused by the many people whose attitudes, values and choices over generations have contributed to the shaping of our society, until its structures seem to have a life of their own and a power over people.

Because it is people who have made the structures as they are, it is people who must change them. Most people, even those who appear to have power, feel that they have very little power or room for choice. (Even the Prime Minister says of her economic policies 'There is no alternative'.) But in fact there are choices though they may be more limited than we might wish. These are not choices that can be made by 'going it alone', but that people must make *in* their roles and relationships within the structures.

I shared, for instance, in a meeting of Teesside industrial managers at which they were talking with the chaplain about their experiences and understandings of 'sin'. They spoke of their temptation to use the ideas of others as if they were their own, to nullify in subtle or less subtle ways the power of bright young colleagues who might challenge their position, to avoid making difficult decisions by 'passing the buck', to let the organization run itself and then to complain that they felt frustrated. These sins are connected with their roles in organizations and have effects on their organization and how other people experience the organization.

These are not things we usually think of as 'sins' and they may seem quite insignificant, but they contribute to the spread of deadness in the firm and to the frustration of other people's hopes and lives.

Concerning these matters there are decisions to be made by each person about his/her own life and behaviour and changes to be made in their relationships within the organization, for instance, in co-operating more creatively with others or changing a style of management.

What I have been describing is a way of getting *inside* the negative aspects of industry. We shall not get rid of sin simply by external changes, but that does not mean that we do not need external changes. Prophecy demands internal *and* external change. The external pressures that lead to negative effects have to be dealt with by structural changes. This means that people, as

well as making judgments about their own sins, have to make
judgments about what is wrong with their organizations, and
should co-operate with others in making choices and changes
that involve policy, structures and politics.

There is no shortage of *criticism* in our society and indeed in
industrial mission. What is missing is the sharpness of *judgment*,
that instead of threshing around with cudgels, knows like a
skilled surgeon, just where to put the knife in in order to heal.
This kind of judgment comes from God (IIeb. 4.12).

I have said that industrial mission in its understanding of
Christian faith operates on a creation model (b). In speaking
about the lack of prophetic judgment, I have pointed to the need
to take into account the reality of evil. In view of the current
experience of people in industry, it may seem unnecessary to
stress that point. Yet what it leads to is the recognition that in
addition to belief in God as Creator we also need to know him as
Saviour. Both creation and salvation are needed. What place has
salvation in the ministry of industrial mission?

'Your faith has saved you' said Jesus (Luke 7.50) to the woman
who was a sinner, to the blind man (Luke 18.42) and to others. In
these cases Jesus did not demand an explicit avowal of faith in
God. Even the blind belief that enables a person to take one step
towards acting on the belief that things can be different,
represents one aspect of salvation. As I have suggested already,
industrial mission does kindle hope and lead people to risk
themselves by acting 'as if . . .' things *could* be different.

In this way they discover that things *can* be different. In taking
such steps people discover new truths about themselves and
about the possibilities of their situation. They *experience* reality in
a new way.

To have faith in the God of Christ's revealing is to go beyond
blind faith, to gain insight into the meaning of what is going on,
to make a conscious decision about one's relationship to the
world and to God's purposes in it and to find new resources in
God. This is why Bishop Hunter related evangelism and
prophecy. Prophecy alerts us to the significance of what is
happening in the world, evangelism questions us about our own
response to the world. Prophecy points us to God's concern for
the salvation of society: evangelism asks about the individual's
part in this. But today evangelism is seen as having nothing to do
with prophecy, and as a result of this separation both are
enfeebled. Can industrial mission discover what it means to be

(socially) prophetic and thereby put evangelism in a proper perspective? Can it overcome its repulsion from a wrong kind of personalism?

A well known definition of evangelism is 'so to present Christ Jesus in the power of the Holy Spirit, that men shall come to put their trust in God through Him, to accept Him as their Saviour, and to serve Him as their King in the fellowship of His Church'.[5]

The problem about this and other evangelistic expressions is that the words do not convey what they are meant to convey. There is in all people some sense of God and none are left entirely without the grace of his spirit, but the ideas people have are often erroneous so that God appears to them to be 'autocratic', 'domesticated', 'churchy' and altogether unworthy of their allegiance. Evangelism is not just a matter of getting people to believe in God, but of what kind of God they are being asked to accept.

This is where prophecy is vital because through its active concern with people and their lives, it opens up new understandings of God; and this is why prophecy and evangelism should not be opposed to each other but belong together.

Industrial mission, in spite of its weaknesses, is I believe one of the church's best possibilities for exercising a prophetic ministry, and for this reason it is also one of the church's best possibilities for performing an evangelistic ministry. We should not under-estimate the difficulties of such a ministry. Expectations and understandings of God in our society are extremely confused. We have to reckon with a past culture that has developed in close relation with religion, but is now overlaid, though not completely displaced by, secular views. Each group and individual has related differently to this process. A series of meetings with some men connected with the Teesside Industrial Mission illustrates this confusion.

At one of the meetings of the mission I had been struck by the fact that during the first part of the meeting chaplains talked about mission, and in the second part laymen talked about money. It appeared that consideration of God was left entirely to the clergy. On raising this matter with two of the lay people present I was invited to help them in an exploration of what the industrial mission meant to them and how they saw Christian faith in its relation to industrial life. They gathered a group of about a dozen men, most of whom were managers and only one of whom was an active member of his church, and we met over a period of about six months. A few quotations from our discussions indicate their understandings of Christian faith:

> One strength of industrial mission is that, while being quite open about its Christian purpose, it has created a platform for all points of view. There is a danger of putting a Christian label on a group for that can create a barrier that makes honest sharing difficult. Now a platform has been developed, the chaplain should help people to break out of traditional industrial constraints and help managers and trade unionists to consider their purposes in a broader philosophical way. He should open up thinking about the whole business of living in industry in the broadest sense. He should meet the lack of satisfaction at all levels and give people courage to work at these problems.

> I feel a need to be more articulate about what I believe but evangelicalism embarrasses me. The problem is heightened by dissatisfaction with my local church.

> Industry makes people lop-sided. (This was illustrated by frustrations felt by managers in their roles especially in a large company.) Christianity aims at wholeness of body and spirit.

> Industrial mission should aim to create a just and democratic society. In order to do this it should find common ground between management and workers – help people to work together, expose prejudices and bring new vision to old problems.

> Industrial mission should identify and handle conflict and understand the consequences of not doing so, open up the issues of the effect of individuals on one another, provide external reference points in value terms, develop the whole person, note industry's impact on the community.

> The above approach derives from a belief in Jesus Christ and from following Him.

The draft paper the group produced for discussion with the chaplains was theologically thin and obviously inadequate. Members of the group were only too conscious of their limitations, but they hoped that their comments might lead to a discussion with the chaplains in the course of which they might gain some clarity. This did not happen. As usual there was difficulty in finding a meeting time that suited everyone and only a few laymen turned up. This was hard on the chaplains who had made a real effort to be present. But worse was to come.

When the laymen presented their paper, the chaplains did not see it as an opening for further discussion of Christian faith. Instead they were shocked by its bland naïvete and dismissed it as totally unrepresentative of industrial mission's true stance. What they did not accept was that, whatever they might have intended, this was in fact what *they* had conveyed through their ministry.

I am not suggesting that much could have been done at that moment beyond helping the group to appreciate what they had achieved (and that is important in itself). The laymen had stayed away because for the time being they had had enough. There would, however, be other occasions and other groups. These might or might not include some of the same people, but they would certainly raise many of the same issues.

These men had picked up from the presence and activities of industrial mission certain signals about the possibilities of God and of Christian faith:

freedom from fixed ideologies, traditions and assumptions:
fuller life than they had yet discovered:
constructive approaches to conflict:
a non-sentimental 'Jesus'.

There is no quick way of resolving the confusions about God and about Jesus that exist for these people, and for many others. To ask for a personal commitment to Christ would be to ask for a commitment to a distorted image of Christ. But that is not to say that nothing should be done. I believe that a true picture of God has to be constructed over a time from a number of different angles. When this is done it is my experience that for some people the picture suddenly falls into place and the penny drops. For the first time they see. . . .

When this happens each person responds in their own way. For someone to say 'I believe in God, what do I do next?', is only a beginning in what should be a lifetime's search for God, and though certain steps can and should be taken in a one-to-one situation of ministry, there is need for some sort of Christian community within which growth can take place. This leads me to a consideration of the church, and to look at this in the light of the place given to the church in the models (a), (b), and (c) (see Chapter III).

It is often pointed out that the church does not have to 'go' to industry by means of industrial mission, for it is already present in the form of the men and women who work in industry. What sort of support can church members give to someone who is feeling his or her way towards Christian faith? Are those who work in industry bringing their faith to bear prophetically on the issues of industry and at the same time living by a deeply personal faith? To what kind of God do they bear witness?

Christians are unevenly spread throughout industry with, for instance, more church members among management and white collar workers than on the shop floor.

As far as their witness in industry is concerned they see this in different ways. For managers open acknowledgment of their church affiliation may be the most obvious form this takes. Many are concerned with the issues of industry and welcome the concern of the chaplains with these matters. They find it difficult, however, to make connections between these issues and their faith or to raise critical questions about industry from the perspective of faith. Church members on the shop floor often display a different attitude. They feel pretty isolated and frequently criticize the chaplains for being more concerned with social issues than with the 'gospel'. Their model of the church is the salvation model (a), that of a separate community, they see the world as evil, and take a judgmental attitude that approximates politically to that of the hard right.

If they meet together it is in order to escape from the world rather than to understand and change the world. It is the existence of such groups that gives rise to the fear of 'holy huddles' and 'Bible thumpers' and the embarrassment about evangelicalism. I do not wish to underestimate the value of the witness that church members are giving in industry in the face of incredible odds – and that is the point – not only has the nature of their task been misunderstood, but what we are up against has not been reckoned with. Many people are expected to 'bear witness' alone and without the necessary theological help.

A number of things have to be done if church members are to exercise their proper ministry in industry. The first thing needed is to deal with their sense of isolation. They too need new understandings and new experiences of what it means to be church.

'Church' for most people means the local church in a particular geographical area. An image of 'church' with which people are familiar is 'The Body of Christ'. Reflection on this image should make it obvious that 'Body of Christ' exists not only as a gathered community of faith but as a dispersed community of service (model (c)). We have no problems in visualizing 'church' as gathered community, but there is little understanding of the shape and needs of a dispersed church. It is this expression of the church that industrial mission seeks to develop. The dispersed mission church needs many different forms. Some of these forms are familiar to us, for instance the church in schools, universities and hospitals. Industrial mission is a more recent expression and although it was set up by the church, many church people see it today as being over against the church. They say 'Why is industrial mission not more closely identified with the (local) church? Why does it not bring more people into the church?'

These criticisms are taken very seriously by the missions and their management committees. So much so that it seemed to me that the missions spent too much time relating to 'the church'. Ordinands were constantly placed for experience with the missions. Both missions ran regular courses for introducing clergy to industry. Most chaplains were attached to churches for Sunday duty, and there were many activities with congregational or ecumenical lay groups.

The assumption behind all this is that, though questions are to be raised about industrial mission, no questions need be asked about the local church. In fact both industrial mission and the local church face the same problem of making faith intelligible in today's world. Their co-operation should be in relation to this shared question to which both have their own contribution to make. If industrial mission's contribution is that of bringing to the rest of the church an understanding of the issues and experiences of industrial life and what this means for believing, it will have *less* time to give to the 'churches' and that time must be used economically and to the point.

Evangelicals claim that people are liberated through a personal experience of Jesus Christ. This claim is not altogether empty, but the fact is that the churches to which such people are joined are of the model (a) type, membership of which is far from being a liberating experience. Industrial mission has rejected this kind of ecclesiastical imprisonment and has been instrumental in releasing people from it. There is no point in being dragged back into a restrictive model of the church.

The real problem is that both sides lack an adequate model of the church. Though industrial mission rejects the model that sees the church only as gathered local church model (a), its chosen model (b) allows the church only a shadowy position. While people operate on different models of the church they will continue to talk at cross purposes, and industrial mission will be criticized on the wrong criteria.

Industrial mission needs to affirm a more positive model of the church that like model (c) sees the need for the church to exist in a variety of forms. Industrial mission's main contribution then would be to create provisional expressions of the church as dispersed in the world. I stress the word 'provisional' for there should be no attempt at a 'grand plan' or imposition of some preconceived structure. The groups must find their own life and develop appropriate structures to support their life. In order to make a start I believe that every chaplain should be working with at least one such group. (This would incidentally undercut another criticism of industrial mission – that of clericalism a matter about which I say more in Chapter VII.)

The purpose of the groups would be to stand in the world for justice and for the God of justice. Because many of those who are most concerned with the issues of industry are not practising Christians, the groups would contain non-Christians as well as Christians. This is of course how things would be in truly missionary enterprises. Each group would make its own decisions and experiments as regards worship, while church members would, in addition to membership of the group, continue to worship in their own churches.

The groups would reflect on their experience in industry in the light of Christian faith. In such thinking someone deeply in touch with Christian tradition would be needed in order that there could be a 'robust' theology. The meetings would not be purely cerebral, but would provide support for people as they respond to their own situations and this would inevitably involve discussion of personal as well as social issues.

A rather more structured example of what I have in mind is the workers' churches that, after many years involvement in industry, have been developed by the Hong Kong Industrial Committee. These churches meet in 'upper rooms' offered by different denominations at peppercorn rent to the Committee, which has (in order to avoid starting a new denomination) affiliated each church to the denomination in whose premises it meets. A recent report gives an insight into the life of one of these churches:

In the process of fighting for justice, safeguarding workers' rights and caring for each other, workers were led to meditate on the gospel. On May 1st, 1983 two workers who confess Jesus Christ were baptized. In the worship they had found liberation for themselves, found an expression of faith in their lives and prayed for the Hong Kong workers. We held bi-weekly Bible studies to explore the relationship between faith and workers' life more deeply. This was a small step towards workers' theology. Both community churches have started a basic course on Christianity for interested workers.[6]

Of course the situations are different and things could not and should not be just like that in Britain. But could not industrial mission in this country use its opportunities more creatively to recover a directness of faith in God through Jesus Christ so that people can discover him as liberator for both themselves as individuals and for society? Can industrial mission take hold of Christian tradition in a more radical way and show how God is involved in our world and work with others in living and thinking this out? If it can do this it will make a much needed contribution to the whole church.

In the next chapter I pursue the question of models of the church from the angle of the local church.

V   Church and World

'Child neglect, old age, violence, boredom, unemployment, lack of transport. . . .' The list of social issues covered several sheets of newsprint and included over one hundred items.

The clergy who had compiled the list were members of an urban ministry course being run for the Middlesbrough Deanery at the instigation of the York Diocesan Ministry Committee.

Looking at the list one member exclaimed in despair:

'What am *I* meant to *do* about it all?'

The church does not know what to *do* about the world because it lacks an adequate model of the church in its relationship to the world and to the purposes of God. This chapter deals with this issue as it emerged in the urban ministry courses which formed one of my main activities.

The first course with which I was involved was in Teesside, where soon after I arrived I was invited to act as theologian for a course in which about twenty clergy came together for three separate weeks spread over a year. The course was repeated at intervals throughout my time as theological consultant. A similar course came out of the Bishop of Durham's Sunderland commission, and, as in the Teesside courses, there were related lay week-ends. Later I was responsible for two courses sponsored by the North-East Ecumenical Group to consider how ministry might relate to the newly constituted county of Tyne and Wear,[1] and a series of consultations took place with the incumbents of the central churches of the smaller towns of Durham Diocese. Finally over a period of two years there was the Middlesbrough Deanery urban exploration already mentioned.

The common element in all these courses was that they aimed to help clergy, and to a lesser extent lay people, to see ministry in relation to society. Although the situations varied a great deal, the underlying theological issues of God/world, church/world were the same. Though I had less involvement in the rural scene, the issue is equally relevant to ministry in the agricultural, industrial and commuter villages that are a feature of the region. In order to be specific I focus on the urban scene.

The city has its own problems in which ministry in the city shares. These problems were present and to some extent recognized by the church long before the riots of Toxteth and Moss Side or the setting up of the Archbishop of Canterbury's Commission on Urban Priority Areas (ACUPA).[2]

The most obvious fact about the city is the large number of people who live in it. The two largest urban concentrations in the North-East Region are Newcastle (278,000) and Middlesbrough (150,000). Both are centres of larger conurbations – Tyneside (which includes Sunderland) has a population of 1,200,000 and Teesside (with the Cleveland hinterland) has 565,000 people.

A second point is that relationships in all cities have developed and been structured on class lines. In the inner city, for instance in Middlesbrough, owners and workers originally lived close to the factories. As time went by the owners and managers moved further and further out. So there is a second 'twi-light' ring of large houses now in decline and with multiple rented accommodation. This is where new arrivals to the city, including overseas immigrants, make their homes. Next, moving outwards from the centre there are the sprawling council estates, consisting of rows and rows of houses with the minimum of public amenities.

These are sharply separated from the estates of private houses. A further ring of more expensive housing is occupied by professional people and others who have sufficient credit to take up large mortgages. Finally there is the 'gin and Jaguar' belt, where the executive class lives in the country villages of North Yorkshire. Each area and each class develops its own separate culture. Work, the basic cause of the divisions, also provides the main means by which people meet across the divisions. This means that those who are most imprisoned in their own group are the women who do not work, that is the wives of the higher echelons.

Two areas of the city that suffer most are the impersonal council estates to which people are moved as houses in the centre are demolished:[3] and the inner city which is inhabited by those who are left behind when the young, the enterprising and the successful move out. They have to endure the noise, mess and disturbance of demolition, with the attendant loss of their local services – and in time the re-building going on all around them. Traffic is a further harrassment with the hurried comings and goings in the morning and at night, and, during the day other people's cars parked in every available space.

A third characteristic of cities is that they can only exist if there is a high degree of social organization. Life in the city is dominated by the institutions that control housing, education, work, social and health services, transport, waste disposal and so on, under the all embracing responsibilities of local and central government.

The individual in the city exists in a social vacuum, in that he does not belong to a natural community. Yet at the same time he is socially controlled by the institutions of the city.

Today, with increasing financial pressure, competition for scarce resources of jobs and services also increases. The fabric of the city deteriorates and there is, especially among the most disadvantaged people, increasing alienation, frustration and anger. This brings into the open, what has always been present, conflict between groups.

The church in the city too has its difficulties. Whereas in the better-off suburban areas church life may flourish, in the inner city and on the council estates it has a struggle to survive.[4]

Negative feelings on the part of the church about its own performance are projected on to the world to re-inforce a theology that, in line with model (a) in Chapter III, sees the world as totally evil. If the church is to minister in and to the world it needs a proper theology of the world and of the church in their relationships with God and with each other.

We have already seen in the models discussed in Chapter III that Christians claim biblical authority for conflicting attitudes towards the world. It is true that the Bible speaks of 'world' in different ways, but these models miss the nature of the distinction. Biblically 'world' may mean:

Human affairs as organized apart from God. This is not as model (a) suggests to say that the creation itself is evil, nor is it a contrast between material and spiritual or everyday and religious affairs. It is a statement that *all* things – people, society, nature *and* our 'spiritual' affairs have been deflected from their true being and purpose and are in need of salvation.

On the other hand 'world' may mean:

The created universe. This is essentially good and is the expression of God in his creativity. This is the position from which model (b) starts, though it fails to see that the world's basic goodness has been marred so that it is now a mixture of good and evil. God is in the world creating *and* redeeming. People are called to co-operate with him in its transformation.

The church's relationship with the world is influenced by which of these understandings of the world predominate. Today the following models of church/world relationships are in evidence:

1. *Sect* In this model the church consists of a community of people gathered *out* of the world. Pressure from a seemingly hostile world drives the church inwards to focus on its own life. In view of this the task of the church is to save individual souls out of an evil world, and the 'end' is to increase the number of the 'saved'. The strength of this model is that it recognizes the power of evil, the need for salvation and that the church has a role in this matter. It challenges its members to a total commitment and, by Bible study and prayer, to a deeper faith. Its weaknesses are, first its negative view of the world. Though it may think it important to *serve* the world, it does not seek to find God *in* the world, but proclaims a 'known' gospel to a 'godless' world. Secondly, the church itself becomes 'world' for its members. Boxing them off from the world, the church inhibits their proper ministry and their full humanity. Thirdly, though it sees that the church has a role in salvation, it misunderstands the nature of salvation and what the church should *do* about it. Many thriving churches today are of this type.

2. *Secular* This model stresses the goodness of the world and in reaction to model (1) plunges into the world for the sake of the kingdom. The strength of this model is its protest against models that, seeing only evil in the world, focus on the church at the expense of the world.

Its weakness is that it does not reckon with the reality of evil and the need for salvation, and by opposing kingdom and church it leaves no place at all for church.

3. *Christendom* Richard Niebuhr described this position as that of 'the Church above society'.[5] The model carries with it echoes of a past situation in which the Western world was the 'Christian' world, and it was assumed that everyone was Christian by birth. The church saw its role as keeping the potential chaos of the

world at bay. Salvation was necessary and salvation was to be found in and through the church.

The church had a recognized position in society and its institutions – education, government, the local community. In these spheres the church, represented by the ordained ministry, had a voice. That is to say the church had power in society. The church saw itself primarily as institution, working through its hierarchy, with laity being of secondary importance. This is the background to the omni-competent parson. The strength of this model lies in the fact that in it the church is concerned with society and with everyone in it.

Its weaknesses lie in the fact that the church does not challenge its members' faith, nor, in its close relationship with society and its desire to keep a broad membership, does it challenge society's practices. As an institution it may survive, but this is at the expense of its faith. It contributes little that is distinctive to society and its members' outlook differs little from that of anyone else.

Today, changes in the church's position in society make this impracticable as a model to follow. In the country or in small towns, where a face-to-face ministry is possible it may still seen useful. But in the urban areas it manifestly does not work. The failure of this model has led many people to choose one of the extreme options (1) or (2).

None of these models gives a satisfactory answer to the question: 'What is the *church* (what am *I*) meant to *do* with the world?'

People are right to point to the weakness and apparent insignificance of the church and to ask:

What is this infinitesimal Christian community supposed to *do* with the vast community of mankind?

To answer this question we must look beyond the church to ask what *God* is doing in and with the world.

Jesus announced God's purposes when he proclaimed the kingdom of God. He demonstrated the nature of God's kingdom as love by dying *for* the *world*. Though Jesus lived a human life, limited as all human lives are by time and place, Christians have no doubt about his *universal* significance.

God is love and his purpose of love is for *all*. The image 'kingdom of God' stands for the goal – love shall overcome lovelessness and all people shall be in communion and community with each other and with God. Then at last we shall see

God as he is – for we shall *be* as he is. All will have been transformed so that the world and humanity truly reflect the likeness of God. In pursuing this purpose God is unreservedly *for* the world.

At first sight this belief raises critical questions for the church in its understanding of its own identity, for it blurs the distinction between church and world. The hard lines of demarcation have been removed. There are not two types of humanity – Christians and others. Humanity is one and all share a common destiny. The emphasis throughout is on the plural *'we'*. God gives *everyone* the possibility of loving others as the instrument of divine salvation. It is in one sense true that 'we are all going the same way', for every person is somewhere on the road of love and all have some experience of love.

In the end all people will be judged, not by whether they have acknowledged Jesus Christ, but by the quality of their love: whether they have fed the hungry, welcomed the stranger, clothed the naked, visited the sick and imprisoned (Matt. 25.31–46).

Many who are not Christians will be surprised to find that they have been following the way of Jesus Christ towards an encounter with Him:

'Lord when did we see thee hungry and fed thee, or thirsty and give thee drink?' (v.37)

In view of this we may well ask 'Why have a church?'.

The church cannot do everything, but there are certain things only the church can do. Christians are not the only people who *do* God's will, but there are certain things that only they can give to the world. The church is not the only instrument of salvation but it is only the church that *knows* what God's purpose is in history. In the light of this knowledge it is the church's task to help the world to understand itself.

This is a different model of the church from those we looked at earlier in this chapter. It does not separate itself from the world (Sect model). It does not lose itself in the world (Secular model) nor does it assume that it has power over the world (Christendom model).

This model is of a church which, by its knowledge of God and his purposes for the world, transforms the world.

Because this is a different model it has implications for every other aspect of Christian faith, and it carries with it the need for different practices. It is at the point of operation that conflict becomes apparent between the different models. In order to illustrate and develop this point I return to the urban ministry courses.

While I was working on a model of transforming the world, members of the courses who had a sect model in their minds understood what I said about involvement in the world as a distraction from their real work of proclaiming the gospel. Those who assumed a Christendom model on the other hand saw the courses as a way of gaining access to and power in society for purposes of their own that did not include transforming society. People not personally involved in the courses, including those who sponsored members, did not see the courses as having any theological content, but simply as useful introductions to aspects of society. If any results were to come from the courses I had to help people find practical ways of ministering *and* at the same time clarify the theological models that would make sense of these practices. I had not simply to give 'tips' about ministry, but also clarify the nature of God's purposes in the world. Theology and practice had to be combined.

My aim of helping the church address itself to a task that concerns God's purposes in the world came into conflict with contrary assumptions about the church's task on quite specific matters: the place of the laity, the significance of institutions and the style of operation. Each of these matters needs some elucidation:

1. My championship of the laity in my job as theological consultant was a constant cause of misunderstanding and conflict. The blindness of so many people to the fact that this was a *theological* issue with implications for the church's whole mission, structure and stance in relation to the world, was, as will appear later, a source of disappointment and frustration in my attempts to help the church become a church *for* the world.

The church exists in two modes which are in vital relation to each other:

in the congregation as community of faith;
in the world as leaven and salt.

While most people recognize the first mode, few understand the second.

Within the congregation (in the first mode), it is assumed that clergy take the lead and that change begins with them, and (perhaps) filters down through them to the laity.

In the world (the second mode) the position is reversed. If the world is to be transformed it is lay people who must be at the forefront, for it is they rather than clergy who can penetrate the world.

If they are not only to penetrate but also change the world, they must contribute a vision that comes out of a faith that has not been quenched by the world. This requires the existence of 'gathered' as well as 'scattered' church. An adequate model of the church will allow for both modes.

All the urban ministry courses I have mentioned were planned for clergy. The lay week-ends that were attached to them were for members of their congregations and represented an attempt to make the point in the face of assumptions to the contrary that clergy cannot effect change by themselves. In spite of the initial difficulties in recruitment, the lay people who attended made the most of the opportunities, and were stimulated to look for ways of continuing their search. Some of the Teesside members joined the Sunday morning theology group (see Chapter VII). The Sunderland members decided they needed more than one weekend's training programme and drew up proposals for a long term training programme to present to the Sunderland Council of Churches and the Deanery Synod. I particularly remember the meeting with the Deanery Synod. A quite modest proposal was submitted suggesting that under the Sunderland Council of Churches a training programme should be planned to cover, say three years, with one or two courses each year to meet the particular needs that members had identified. Crowded out by other agenda items, the group's proposals were met by counter proposals and descriptions of the 'wonderful' lay training already going on or projected in certain parishes. Perhaps this was predictable but it was sad to see this kind of reaction to a serious attempt by lay people to take some responsibility for their own development.[6] This was not the only time that I experienced the force of the church's resistance to change.

Lay members for the urban courses were recruited from their congregations by the clergy, but church members are not the only people who contribute to the transformation of the world. For this task we must also look for colleagues from among people who may not call themselves Christians, but who are deeply concerned with what happens in the world. This requires a strategy akin to that of industrial mission that starts *outside* the congregation. Christians should expect to learn something from people outside the church and from the world, for God's spirit is at work throughout the world and in all people.

2. The second theological/practical factor that needs comment is that of institutions. The church's individualistic theology inhibits it from seeing the importance of the structures of society. Why, for instance, should the church have any interest in the formation of a new county if its only concern is with individual souls? One purpose of the urban ministry courses was to help members discover the significance for their ministry of the social structures.

The Tyne and Wear course began with a bus tour of the whole county in which members could see their own patch on a wider canvas, and ask questions about the county itself: What values are implicit in the use of resources? Which areas gain and which lose out? Who makes decisions in whose interest?

In order to answer these questions we invited people who held responsibility in the institutions of the county – local government, education, industry, to talk with us about their jobs, their hopes and their frustrations.

By listening to people's stories it was possible to realize for instance, that temptation exists in institutional forms. For trade unionists and local councillors, it has its own specific manifestations – getting out of touch with those they represent, using power and using people for one's own ends, going it alone, cynicism. In the same way sin is not just an individual matter, but, as we saw in the last chapter, is in the structures of society, and is more complex than the black-and-white caricature that presents itself for our judgment from outside.

To be concerned with structures means accepting the reality of conflict and entering the controversial political arena. It means that in anything we do we place ourselves on one side or the other. In the urban courses for instance, by introducing members to people with power in the institutions, we *chose* to look at the city from their perspective. A different view would have come from the unemployed young people who hang about the shopping centres. Any hint of conflict is deeply offensive to church people, but if we remember that God's reconciliation is based on justice we should not fear the 'grey' areas of life where justice and reconciliation are relative terms. To work with institutions requires specific skills. The church no longer has the power it used to have and it should not try to seize power. It must work by making relationships, gaining trust over a long period and by identifying and getting to grips with the issues. It should neither ignore nor take a negative attitude to institutions, but, recognizing that institutions share in the imperfection of humanity, should be positive about the need for good institutions.

Beyond the obvious conflict between an individualistic and a corporate view of salvation, this matter raises the issue of how success is to be measured and with what kind of time-scale we should work. The church is not unlike the politicians, it *needs* success, results are expected quickly and heads (votes) have to be counted. An individual *may* undergo an instant conversion (though for most people this too is a long process), but change in an institution usually takes generations. Numbers of new church members may be counted but changes in institutions cannot easily be measured.

3. The third theological/practical factor concerns a change of style. One reason for resistance to change is the recognition that a change of outlook carries with it the need for change in everything else. A belief that God calls us to work with him in the world demands from those, who at present focus their ministry on the gathered church, a change in their style of ministry. Two matters of style in particular must be mentioned:

Ministry in the world must be conducted by *dialogue* rather than proclamation: and by *co-operation* rather than in isolation.

Dialogue is a problem for clergy who are more used to talking than to listening. In one of the Teesside courses members returned from a meeting with local councillors in some distress. They had listened for some time to the councillors' description of the questions that concerned them, and had then asked 'What do you expect from the church?' It was the councillors' answer that caused the distress, for they said quite bluntly 'Nothing'.

Christians and clergy in particular feel a compulsive need to give, and especially to give 'the gospel' to others. But in dialogue our first need is to recognize our own poverty and the fact that before we can give we have much to receive. This sense of uselessness is hard to endure, but it should be a salutary step towards repentance for the 'busyness' that stops us from understanding the deeper causes of disturbance, sin and suffering in society.

Regarding co-operation – the present tradition of the church
and the assumption in clergy training is that the clergyman will
'run his own show'. This simply does not work in urban society,
and does much to account for the frustration and isolation felt by
many clergy. The clergyman, mentioned at the start of this
chapter, looking at the list of social issues did not have to ask
'what am *I* meant to do about them?' Rather he should have asked
'*Who* is already tackling these issues and how can I co-operate
with them?'

We should not underestimate the resistance there is to any
kind of sharing even between the clergy themselves. Before the
Middlesbrough course started I came up against this resistance.

I had prepared a draft paper for the use of the course planning
committee. In it I tried to show the need for co-operation between
the clergy:

> Patterns of relationship spread across the whole town. No
> parish is a self-contained community. Each parish represents
> one section of the community whose interests may be at
> variance with those of another area. People travel from one
> part of the town to another to go to school, work and so on.
> Pressures on people in one place often come from what goes on
> elsewhere; for instance pollution spreads across parish
> boundaries, housing and educational policies are decided in
> one place and affect people in another area. A ministry to the
> whole person and the whole community must be seen within a
> town-wide perspective.[7]

One member of the planning group, a layman, on receiving the
draft wrote a long and angry letter to the chairman:

> The preamble has some gratuitous comments. . . . The
> approach is too radical, too circumstantial, too environmental.
> The approach does not sufficiently respect a man's sense of in-
> dependence, self-sufficiency, omni-competence and account-
> ability-to-heaven-only.

He ended his letter by suggesting that the authority of the
clergyman is undermined by any suggestion that he has not got
all the answers, and a side-swipe at me as a lay person, a woman
and an outsider:

> Can credibility in the area of 'helping' be maintained while
> telling a man to go out and learn more about the patch he has

been cultivating for years, even if the need for this is apparent to third parties?

These practical illustrations of different approaches to – lay people, institutions and styles of operation may seem slight, but they are significant of deep theological differences. In view of this confusion it is not surprising that clergy feel overwhelmed by the world, do not know what to *do* with the world and find it easier to *do* things with the church. But concentrating on the church will not do the work of the church for the work of the church is to do with the world.

The church, as I have indicated in model (c) in Chapter III, maintains the memory of Jesus of Nazareth. Jesus revealed God's purposes for the world and he is the clue by which we understand the world and what we have to do in the world. Christians do not look *back* to the historical life of Jesus as a matter of self-edification, but in order that they may make sense of the *present* and that the path *ahead* may be illuminated.

If we misunderstand God we shall misunderstand the church and its task. What kind of church we have depends on what kind of God we believe in.

To despise and fear all that is natural and human shows that we do not believe that in the humanity of Jesus God committed himself to humanity. Then we shall have no stomach for involvement in the world, and our church will be busy with its own life rather than being active 'to do good, seek justice, correct oppression, defend the fatherless, plead for the widows' (Isa. 1.17).

If we go in the opposite direction and shrug our shoulders, accepting the world as it is and assuming that things cannot be changed, our church will simply reflect the life and outlook of the world, and our God is no more than a cipher.

But if, following Jesus Christ, we are passionately concerned for the suffering of the world, we shall be compelled to be involved in the world. In that case the church we create will be a church that supports us in that involvement. By reflection on the world and on Christian tradition it will help us to discover what God is calling us to *do* about the sufferings of the world. By encouragement of each other in our varied callings, by the eschatological fellowship and worship of the church and by discernment of its presence here and now in the world, we shall have a foretaste of the kingdom of God. The God witnessed to in this case is one who is himself involved in the world and who on the cross died *for* the world.

What such a church should look like in practice and structure is the subject of Chapters VII and VIII. In Chapter VI, I ask 'How does God complete his purposes in the world? How does he think we can contribute to his kingdom?'

VI Good News to the Poor?

How does God save? From what and for what does he save us? What is the part of Christians and of the church in the process of salvation?

The word 'salvation' has for many people lost its edge, and is seen to refer only to some inward change in individuals. As one way of opening up the meaning of 'salvation' many people today prefer the word 'liberation'. A new style of theology in Latin America is known as 'liberation theology'. This chapter discusses what the church in Britain may learn from this theology for its own strategy and practice. It concludes that it would be wrong to adopt liberation theology in its Latin American form, but that we can learn much from it that can help us to develop our own indigenous theology.

Liberation theology developed in South America in response to a situation of poverty and oppression and its concern is with the poor and the oppressed. (We should note that the situation of most people in the world is nearer to that than to the real though different disadvantages of our own country.)

By using the word 'liberation' theologians have opened up the traditional idea of 'salvation' by indicating a relationship between salvation and creation. (This leads beyond the polarization of the two models in Chapter III). The inter-connection between salvation and creation, and between God's kingdom and man's co-operation with God in the building up of the world, are developed by the liberation theologian, Miguez Bonino:

> Creation is the installation of a movement; it is an invitation and a command to man to create his own history and culture, creatively to transform the world and make it into his own house and to explore the configurations of human relationships available to him.

When the realm of creation is understood in the terms we

have sketched, the soteriological notions of sin and redemption
gain a new meaning . . . Jesus Christ does not come to
superimpose a different, transcendent, or celestial reality on top
of the realm of nature and history, but to reopen for man the will
and power to fulfil his historical vocation . . . to be man.[1]

In liberation theology salvation has three aspects. It is:
   through history,
   from sin, and
   for communion with each other and with God.
The word 'history' needs some explanation. It does *not* mean
the dates and events from the past that are the subject of 'history'
lessons at school. History is an interpretation of the *meaning of
events*. Where there is no belief in a meaning or pattern in life,
there is no history – life is just one thing after another, a cycle of
birth, life and death.
   Israel saw God as a God of history because he gave meaning to
her life. It was Israel's belief in God that enabled her not only to
see meaning in events but to *actualize* that meaning by taking a
hand in shaping events through which she became a people.
   There are many different views of what purpose and pattern
there is in events, and on this matter there are basic differences
among Christians. A disabling and widespread *misunderstanding*
among Christians is that religion is not concerned with 'secular'
events at all.
   The liberation theologians contest this view by basing their
understanding of salvation on the Exodus story. Using this story
they assert that God saves *through* history.
   Although we do not know exactly what happened, we see in
the Exodus events, beginning from the call of Moses, God *offering*
salvation, and people having to risk themselves to respond in
action to that offer. Israel could only take the steps she did
because she believed in a God who liberates. The theme of God
saving through history runs right through the Bible, so that Jesus'
death is spoken of in terms of his Exodus (Luke 9.31). Throughout history God is all the time calling people to participate in
history so that it becomes saving history. This is not to suggest
that there are instant solutions. Salvation is a long process in
which there are many set-backs, as faith becomes clouded and
weak and as people lose hope and turn back. Nor am I suggesting
that humankind saves itself, but that we may accept or reject
God's salvation. All the time God is in history and in every

situation he is offering us choices which lead towards life or towards death.

A Marxist interpretation of history claims that the essential choices people have to make are to do with external and structural changes in society. Internal change in people's dispositions, it claims, will follow external change. In contrast, Christians, while they agree that there is need to tackle the things that are wrong in society, see the root cause of 'the sin in the structure' to be in people. They therefore see a need for internal as well as external change, that is for salvation *from sin*.

If people are to take responsibility for history, they must also take responsibility for their own behaviour and dispositions that have deadly or life-giving effects in history. Through Jesus Christ God saves us from sin by 'the forgiveness of sins, namely, man's freedom in God's grace to take up again, in whatever circumstances and after whatever failure and destruction, the work committed to him in creation'.[2]

Salvation is not only about what we need to be saved *from*, but what we need to be *saved for*. The positive purpose of salvation is to free people *for communion*. By co-operation with God in solidarity with others, people are enabled to create a society in which it is possible to be in communion with each other, and with a transcendent God who, because he can free us from sin and overcome its effects in our society, makes communion a possibility.

What can we in Britain learn from all this? To take liberation theology over wholesale would be to deny its first tenet. It is not a theology that deals with timeless generalizations but with specific matters of time and place. It starts at the point where people identify *their* issues where *they* are, and by seeing these issues in the light of faith try to respond to them in faith.

So the first lesson we must learn is that we must start, not in Latin America or anywhere else, but where *we* are here and now in Britain. We must ask 'Who are the poor and the oppressed in this country?' and, as I am trying to be specific, 'Who are the poor in the North East?' I have suggested that in spite of its contrasts the whole region is disadvantaged. For the purpose of this discussion I highlight some groups that are especially oppressed: working women, unskilled manual workers and workers in traditional industries such as shipbuilding, steel and coal whose life and work is threatened.

I pick out these groups not only because they are comparatively poor in financial terms, but because they also suffer from another form of deprivation – powerlessness.[3] Certain groups in society have power over others and appear to them as oppressors. For working women it is men who have the right to treat them as inferiors, for the poor and the unemployed the 'powers that be' are represented by the social services, for those working in the traditional heavy industries of the region it is the government and the boards of the nationalized industries who, it appears, can at the stroke of a pen, deprive them of the only way of life they know.

The needs of working women are beginning to receive some belated attention, but the ideal of womanhood projected by the church is still that of wife and mother. Industrial mission, which reminds the church of its responsibilities towards the world of work, was set up to serve working *men*. Only now, as a result of the appointment of several women chaplains, is it slowly waking up to the fact that today it is working men and working women who need their attention.

In my role as theological consultant I saw my job as not only helping people to do the tasks they had set for themselves, but as pointing to areas of work which they were not touching. As far as the Teesside Industrial Mission was concerned I felt that they should be doing more to serve the needs of women, and in order to explore how this might be done, I took a job for a short period in a factory that employed a large number of women. I had managed to get just four weeks clear for this project, and though I realized that little could be achieved in so short a time, I believed that through this experience I might discover how longer term work could be undertaken. It seemed to me that the industrial mission might employ someone to work in a rather different way by actually spending a large part of their time as a worker.[4]

My few weeks in the factory gave me plenty of food for thought. I had intended to spend the whole time in a potato crisp factory, but had to change to a calculator factory as, at the end of my first day packing crisps, I along with fifty other temporary workers was given twenty-four hours' notice of redundancy.

I was sorry to leave the crisp factory. It offered me so many opportunities. It employed 1500 workers, most of them were women, and they had gained a reputation for being 'rough', though of course people there as anywhere else varied. There was a certain volatility, as I learned on my first day when most of the workers walked out because it was too hot. An impromptu meeting was held in the yard and we spent several hours sitting in the canteen until the matter was settled. Trouble also arose over the redundancies and I was asked to join in a protest. At lunch time I had not recognized the woman in overalls and cap as a member of my local church, until she spoke to me asking (uncharacteristically) 'Are you slumming?' I knew her and her husband as members of the church congregation, but what did it mean to be a Christian in this place and what here constituted Christian witness? I did not have time to explore these questions.

The workers at the calculator factory were on the surface more 'respectable'. I had no feeling there that I was 'slumming'. These women were like me just earning their living, though of course there was a mixture of types. An industrial chaplain worked in this firm and his one visit while I was there made me realize (from the receiving end) how little he could accomplish from that position.

Soon after, as part of their attempt to make a contribution to industrial life, this the Girls' Friendly Society offered to finance the appointment of a woman chaplain to the Teesside Industrial Mission team. This seemed to me to present an opportunity for the kind of appointment that I had been exploring. I presented to the team a draft job description.

This proposed that the appointee should pick up the task that I had been exploring. Her aim would be to work *with* people for a period, with a view to seeing things as they see them, not imposing questions, but discovering insights and leadership within the situation. She would, as far as possible, with the people involved, reflect on their experience in the light of Christian faith and aim to discover how Christian faith can illuminate life for people at 'shop floor' level.

As far as the structure of the job was concerned, periods of work experience would be interspersed with periods of non-work. This is different from the worker-priest concept in that it is not a life-long commitment to work, but a way of gaining and renewing a perspective and a commitment.

My job description was accepted and in the summer of 1977 a young woman, who had just finished her training at theological college, started work with the mission.

After a general induction period she worked from September until Christmas in the calculator factory where I had been for a short time.

An incident frankly recorded in her report on this period reveals one of the main difficulties the church has in its relationship with 'the poor'. I refer to the gulf between the reality of the situation and the expectation of what it means to be a minister of the gospel. She wrote:

> I was putting jackscrews on to the machines when I dropped a pile of screws and washers and nearly swore aloud, which seemed to break the ice with the girls I was working with. For the first time they began to ask me questions about my job, God and the resurrection all at once, and the combined effect of the dropped screws, the depth of the questions and a build-up of calculators made me feel completely out of my depth and unable to convey anything of what I might have wanted to say, and I felt absolutely overwhelmed. This contributed to my wanting to leave and exacerbated niggling doubts as to my vocation and my ability ever to be effective as a chaplain. A few days later . . . the feelings of helplessness, of resentment and frustration were back with me. The next day I found that I could not face a whole day of the same situation, went to the toilets for a break and a smoke, but could not bring myself to go back on the line. This stress produced physical symptoms of giddiness, slight sickness and a temperature, and after being sent to the sickroom for two hours before lunch I was sent home. . . . The doctor diagnosed a chill, yet signed me off for a total of three weeks, during which I was very depressed. This was about half-way through the total period. On returning to the factory . . . I had no further 'crises' for the remainder of the work experience.[5]

I do not want to build too much on this one story, but it is typical of other examples I could give. It seems to me that something has gone seriously wrong when theological training leads people to believe that at the end they should have ready answers to every question.

If in addition these 'answers' are couched in traditional churchy language they will not convey much to most people.

If we always have to be right, we can hardly sympathize with those who are only too conscious that they are *not* all right.

If we have no reverence for human beings in all their ordinary humanness we shall fail to have reverence for God.

If we have an image of ourselves as being 'in control' of our situation, our image of God will be different from that of a God who revealed himself in powerlessness on the cross.

In this particular case there were additional difficulties. It was obviously a mistake to link an attempt to develop a new style of work with that of a first female appointment, and the appointee naturally suspected that it was because she was a woman that she was asked to do a 'lay' job. She was moreover straight from college and lacked previous experience. But the fact remains that the way ministers are trained, the expectations of ministry and the theological perspective they acquire does not prepare them for the task of helping 'the poor' to discover the good news of the gospel.

My second example concerns the weakness of the church's contact with the unskilled manual workers and its blindness to the possibilities of what is already happening and to what more it might do. In 1976 the Bishop of Durham (John Habgood) raised the question of the church's lack of contact with working class people at his extended staff meeting of which I was a member. I maintained that there were some signs of hope and that the best way forward would be to build on them. I offered to explore what was hopeful in this respect in the Diocese and to present my findings at a later meeting.

During the next few months I visited parishes in the Diocese which had more or less working class congregations and presented a brief paper to the Bishop's meeting in February 1977.

In this paper I set the context of the discussion by pointing to two ways of defining 'working class' – the political and economic or the cultural, that is to say, a style of life. I then gave a short bibliography before describing some attempts in the Diocese to meet the problem. These included a 'problem' council estate where local clergy were co-operating with social workers, the work of the Stockton Community Chaplain, the industrial missions and a working class parish with a vigorous evangelically minded vicar where the congregation was growing rapidly. I was well aware of the glaring weaknesses in each of these things, but I could also see that in each there was something that could be of help in tackling the gap between the church and the working classes. Perhaps the greatest need was for understanding and support for these frail enterprises. The parish clergyman, for instance, was carrying an immense burden and it seemed to me it was only a matter of time before he broke down – then what would be the future of that piece of work? Why will the church never build on what is already there?

As was usual in this particular meeting of senior churchmen I met with a negative response. I had tried to show the hopeful signs, but they were quick to point out that these things were 'not as good as I had suggested'.

In fact I was not saying that these things were perfect, I was simply saying 'These things are there, let's build on them'. But they had only seen the failures and because they were looking in the end for super-men, they were bound to despair and I was bound to get a negative response. My faith leads me to recognize that we are *all* fallible, but that God can use us and God can make something of our often feeble efforts. This the people at the meeting did *not* believe.

My faith leads me to believe that God calls us *all* to share in his purposes and to 'increase in the knowledge of God' (Col. 1.10). These people did not believe that 'uneducated, common men' (and women) (Acts 4.13) were capable of theological thought.

My third illustration concerns people working in traditional heavy industry – in this case in coal mining. It points to the potential in such people to respond to hopes for liberation.

Travelling westwards from Durham there is evidence in the deserted mining rows of the fate of communities when pits are closed. Nor is it only the coal mines that are at risk. In 1980 Consett Steelworks was closed with the loss of 4000 jobs. The effect was not only to cut off the life blood of a thriving town but to remove the only source of employment for many surrounding villages. The most tragic aspect of this is that people expect nothing better. There has been acquiescence and an absence of anger.

But things are changing. In 1985, coal miners returned to work after the longest industrial strike in the history of this country. The fact that they went back without achieving any of their objectives was claimed as a victory by the government. But this does not mean that nothing was changed. The mining communities learnt some hard lessons about solidarity in struggle. Women, who had scraped, managed, run feeding centres and stood on picket lines, discovered their own worth and will not easily return to a life confined to the home. The NUM President, ebullient as ever, stated that a main achievement of the strike is the politicization of young miners.[6]

If this suggests at least the beginnings of some kind of hope for liberation, can the church learn anything from it?

To suggest in church circles that 'ordinary' working people might reflect on what is happening to them in life as a starting point for theology is to be told: 'No one is interested in what is going on around them, and the idea that people should give serious thought to such things is "middle-class intellectualizing". "Ordinary" people should not be bothered with such questions.' It is of course true that active support for CND, prisoners of conscience, disengagement from South Africa, feminism, checks on the powers of multi-national corporations – is not typical of most people in this country whether they are Christians or not. In the face of this seeming indifference it is easy to give up hope. In this respect the secular example of the miners' strike has lessons for us.

First, it shows the potential of 'ordinary' people to take hold of ideas which change their stance towards life. Yorkshire miners in the early 1960s were not noted for their militancy (nor were they 'middle class intellectuals'!). Today many of them have become politically aware – and this for them does not mean simply following Arthur Scargill, but making up their own minds about where they stand. If awareness of meaning in their lives can be developed by Scargill among miners, it can be developed by the church among 'ordinary' people.

But the church does not develop people's awareness of themselves, of the world or of God. It gives them homilies and snippets, not even milk let alone the meat of the gospel. It does not put anything like the thought, effort, planning and persistence into the education of the laity as Scargill does into the education of the miners. I can only conclude that it is because whereas Scargill believes in his cause, the church does not believe in hers.

I knew that it would take just as long to develop a Christian awareness as it did to produce political awareness. During twelve years as theological consultant I worked and planned to lay down proper plans and strategies by which this could happen. But it will take more than twelve years to come to fruition. It appears now, that no one sees the importance of carrying forward what was begun with a great deal of sweat and tears (see Chapter VIII).

Secondly, the mining example shows the need to link events to interpretation and theory to practice. Scargill and his companions used what happened in the industry as a focus for making their philosophy explicit. The threat of a pit closure, for instance, was not seen as an isolated incident, but as part of a pattern, which included the long term plans of the NCB, and, in Marxist categories, the wider threat to the working class. The relevance of the event to each individual was pointed out, and what they should *do* about it. Scargill and his colleagues were convinced of the need for a coherent theory and expected people to grapple with facts and ideas. Scargill did not do all this alone. There was a group within which leadership was not always in the same person. It was not a closed group for it spread its thinking throughout the coalfield, and made a point of 'bringing on' those who showed promise. They never considered that their education was completed but continued to engage in an action/reflection process, which in Marxist terms is called 'praxis'.

Christians also have a theory (theology) by which they interpret what is happening in life. We need to engage in a similar way with people at the points where life puts questions to them and help them to understand these happenings in the light of Christian faith. Many people, besides those who are caught up in the trauma of the mining industry, desperately need a theoretical basis upon which to respond to their situation, but most of our theology has little bearing on the realities of life.

Thirdly, Scargill and company were not deflected from their purpose by their many set-backs. They did not expect easy victories but carried on even when things in the industry were going smoothly and no one seemed interested in what they were saying. They did this because they *believed* in their cause. In contrast many of the activities of the churches take place in such an ad hoc, disjointed way, without long term aims or strategy that they suggest a total lack of belief in the potential of people or the purposes of God.

I am not suggesting that a doctrinaire ideology is to be equated with vision nor that just any vision will do. A vision that is not true to reality only leads to disappointed hopes. If the problem with Scargill's vision was that it bore less and less relation to reality, the problem with the church is that it operates without having *any* compelling vision.

In this example I have not drawn out the negative lessons. There was, during the miners' saga, plenty of skull-duggery and manipulation. Many miners do not agree with Scargill (to politicize people does not guarantee that they will agree with you); the miners were misled. I do not justify any of these things, but use this example primarily to make the point that among 'ordinary' people attitudes have been changed and social awareness has been developed.

I must now return to the question of what we in Britain may learn from liberation theology, bearing in mind that we cannot adopt it just as it is, but must develop what is appropriate to our situation.

I have already said that we should start where we are. In Britain I believe that means as it does in Latin America, having a bias to the poor. Their need is the greatest and it is, as Emilio Castro remarked, 'the poor of the world who are most likely to be deprived not only of bread but of the gospel'. This chapter has illustrated the difficulty the church in Britain has in having any sort of contact with the poor. Our difficulties are compounded by the social and cultural divisions of our society, and by the fact that theology has become imprisoned in one particular culture. Theology itself needs to be liberated. This need is all the more urgent when we note that even in the North East many of the poor of the inner cities belong to other faiths!

But if we give priority to the poor, as I believe we should, we need to ensure that this focus does not harden into an ideology that distorts. We must constantly check our practice against that of Jesus, who in the society of his time did not totally align himself with any one sectional interest but cut across the divisions that existed. In his openness to the poor he stepped outside the Jew's religious exclusiveness, but he also had contact with the rich. In the early church 'not many were powerful, not many were of noble birth' (I Cor. 26), but there were some who were both rich and powerful. The new thing about the church was that it cut across the social spectrum to include rich and poor, Jew and Gentile, male and female, and in the power of the resurrection created new kinds of social relationships in a new kind of society.

A second lesson to be learnt from liberation theology is to see salvation in *all* its aspects: *through* history, *from* sin and *for* communion. In Latin America there was at first emphasis on the historical/political aspect. More recently there has been development in consideration of issues of spirituality.[7] In Britain we start from the opposite pole and now need to overcome our fear of the historical/political aspect of salvation. The church should make critical intervention and comment on political affairs at all levels of our national life and it should affirm that this is integral to Christian faith. Some people are getting involved in the social/political arena but a problem, to which I return later, is that we are still uncertain about how this relates to the gospel.

Thirdly we need to develop our own indigenous theology *with* people who share a common experience of life. Here we come up against the problem of the vast difference in our two situations. In Latin America most people are in an obvious state of deprivation and oppression and one does not have to look far to find common experience. In Britain, though there is real poverty and oppression the general impression is that of not being too badly off. In Latin America most people are traditionally Catholic, which is not to say that they are all articulate and practising church members, but that they share a common heritage. This means that the basic communities within which liberation theology is being developed are natural communities with common issues and a common religious background. In Britain church congregations are on the whole eclectic and unrepresentative of the communities within which they are set. Members do not share common experience of life at a deep level, and the religious background in Britain is more varied and tenuous. It seems to me that if liberation theology is to be a truly indigenous growth here, it must start in communities that come into being *outside* the present church congregations.

There are resources both inside and outside our congregations. Let us look *outside* for a moment.

If Christians would only *listen* to the concerns of the women in the factories, the coal miners on strike, the managers who are responding to economic pressures, the people living under conditions of multiple deprivation, the many people who from other than Christian motivation are trying to relieve their condition – they would discover a completely different agenda from that of the church. These things are not discussed as a matter of urgency in the church, but they are the priorities of *people* and they should be the priorities of the church. To look outside is to change our priorities.

Conversation within the church is conducted within unspoken limits and conventions, and in a language that sets a gulf between religious and ordinary talk. The industrial chaplain for instance who was doing her work experience in the factory wanted to talk about 'God' and 'resurrection', but she was unable to do so until the women gave her a signal by using the 'right' words. Looking outside the church can help us understand our faith as having reality in everyday life.

Nor is this simply a matter of discovering how *we* Christians can give *our* faith to others. We need to *learn* from those who are outside the church 'to attend to the voices, the experiences and the spiritual riches of the "poor" in our midst'.[8]

Among the many people in the North East who are giving practical help to those who suffer in our society, there are many Christians. Their humanity has driven them into action and they often feel that they do this not because, but in spite of the dictates of their faith. Because they have been nurtured in a Christianity in which religion and life are separate, they may be able to give practical help but they cannot bring people to total liberation. They may help people to take hold of their own lives but they are unable to help them to discover God in their lives. They may reveal themselves as caring people but they do not reveal God as a caring and liberating God. In sensing a choice between their faith and the call of humanity they have opted for humanity. The tragedy is that by thus opposing Christianity and humanity they not only lose God but also lose the possibility of helping to create a truly human world. For it is in God that we may find both the vision and the resources for being human.

Reinhold Niebuhr has this to say about how the insights of Christian religion have been perverted by the more comfortable and privileged classes, who have:

> sentimentalized them to such a degree, that the disinherited, who ought to avail themselves of their resources, have become so conscious of the moral confusions which are associated with them, that the insights are not immediately available for the social struggle in the Western world. If they are not made available, Western civilization, whether it drifts towards catastrophe or gradually brings its economic life under social control, will suffer from cruelties and be harrassed by animosities which destroy the beauty of human life. Even if justice should be achieved by social conflicts which lack the spiritual elements of non-violence, something will be lacking in the character of the society so constructed.[9]

As Niebuhr indicates, in God as he is revealed in Jesus Christ there are insights about being human which are *not* part of our secular culture. In the life, death and resurrection of Jesus Christ there is a specific *way* to be followed. In the presence of the Holy Spirit power is available to put these insights into practice. The promise is that God himself will bring the kingdom, but it is the will of God to do his work in the world *through* human beings . . . that means us. God gives us the insights, the way and the power to make a real and practical contribution to the kingdom.

If we are to respond to this offer we need a theology that engages with the issues of life, an indigeneous theology that starts from the human situation, that enables us to see that the concerns of humanity are the concerns of God, and that puts theory and practice together. This is the kind of theology with which I am concerned. It is eminently practical for it gives urgency and direction to our action.

If the church is to take these lessons to heart and *act* upon them, it will require quite different strategies and structures. This is the subject of the next two chapters.

VII Theology for Everyone

The over-riding aim of all that I did as theological consultant was to help people grasp the fact that God is for them. A response to this offer requires a belief in God, that is to say it requires theology. Belief is a response of the whole person and it is acquired within the life of a community. It is not simply an intellectual matter, but it does involve a process of thinking in which each person reflects on their experience of life and how this relates to God. This process is 'theology' and theology is essential to every Christian and to the church. Nor is theology confined to the church. Most people, whether they call themselves Christian or not, have some sort of theology, insofar as they have beliefs or assumptions about life, the world and God. Technically the word 'theology' means knowing and articulating beliefs about *God*, but we should not interpret the concept too narrowly. Everyone has some sense of the transcendent (though they may not call this God), and everyone has some feeling and searching after what is beyond their immediate grasp. Though this may not strictly be called 'theology' it is the basic material of theology.

The point is that theology is natural to human beings. The problem is that theology has been hijacked by the 'professionals'. The practice of theology is surrounded by a mystique and a language that excludes lay people; and in popular usage 'theology' means having no bearing on the realities of life.

My aim was and is to overcome the blockages and to get theology flowing throughout the life of the church and beyond. My efforts were constantly thwarted as I was told 'Lay people should not be bothered with these matters', 'Middle class intellectuals may be interested, but theology is not for "ordinary" people'.

In this chapter I describe what theology is, why it is essential to every Christian and to the church, and, by examples from my own experience, the possibilities and problems of getting theology going.

There are two conflicting views of what theology is:

The popular view is that theology is a body of doctrine based on the Bible and handed down from generation to generation. In this view the church through its ministers guards and transmits the tradition. Theology is a matter of knowing the facts and getting them right.

The opposing view is that theology is a way of understanding life from the perspective of faith in God as he has made himself known in Jesus Christ. This cannot be learnt by rote but is a participative and life-long process of reflection on the realities of life in the light of Christian tradition.

The first view is static in that there is no new knowledge of God beyond that which has been revealed once and for all in Jesus Christ.

The second view is dynamic in that it expects God to make himself known in new ways in a changing world.

Arguments about the nature of theology are not, as some people make out, unimportant, for they concern differences about God:

Is God, as the first view suggests, bound to the past, so that in order to know him we must continually look *back*? or

Is God a living God who makes himself known in life *today*? If this is so every believer has a unique knowledge of God to share with others.

Is God only concerned with attitudes of mind? or does he call us to co-operate with him in the transformation of the world? If this is so everyone needs to discover what *their* part may be; and lay people who live most fully in the world will have a critical part to play in the total theological process.

To start from the fundamental belief that God is to be known *in* life clearly demands a different approach to theology from that which is usual. This is not just a matter of method, though many people try to dismiss it as such. The issue is about God and belief in a living God who is active in the world. Clergy (and others) may continue to preach about God in church. Scholars may continue to lecture about God in the university. This is necessary, but it is only part of a theological task which is concerned with the discovery of and response to God in life. This is the burden of this book and upon this point I cannot compromise.

It is our basic differences about God that determine our methodological approach: The starting point for the first view is the Bible, Christian tradition and the doctrinal concepts of creation, redemption and so on. In the second view the starting point is human experience. The process in the first view involves the transmission of what is known about God; in the second it is a search for the unknown God. The purpose of the first view is indoctrination and socialization into the life of the church, in the second it is liberation for the work of the kingdom. In the first clergy take the lead, in the second, because it is concerned with changing the world, lay people are crucial.[1]

One aspect of the current slant on theology must be taken to heart. Those who say that theology is only for the 'middle-classes' are right as far as *their kind of theology* is concerned. There is a division of cultures in our society, that may roughly be termed middle-class/working class, that concerns the way people learn. This is not a difference in intellectual capacity, but a difference between those, who as a result of a particular kind of education, have (to some extent) learned to think in *abstract* terms, and those who think in *concrete* terms. Theology is currently practised at a highly abstract level, and all of us who have undergone formal theological training have been infected with this approach. Yet pictures, stories, concrete realities and practical responses are much closer to the biblical mode of expression. We only have to look at what Scargill did with the miners to realize what is possible for 'ordinary' people. There is no lack of capacity for theological thought among 'working class' people. It is our *way* of doing theology that is wrong.[2]

I do not claim to have solved this problem in my own practice. In earlier chapters I have described activities in which I was alongside the 'poor'. These people had little time for 'meetings', but within the informal settings real communication about the meaning of their lives took place. The examples I give in this chapter are of more structured work and the people involved, though they were not all 'middle-class' were articulate and able to cope with 'meetings'.

The basic problem concerns all lay people. Today the very notion of what a lay person is has been perverted A 'good' lay person is seen as one who is active in the church. The theological training of these lay people is controlled by the clergy, who socialize them into sharing their own concerns, assumptions and attitudes. 'By inventing the special offices of readers, deaconesses, elders, and others, lay persons whose ministry is out of the common run are drawn into the status and mores of ordained or quasi-ordained ministry.'[3]

All this is built upon a misunderstanding of what a lay person is. Contrary to the above notion 'the lay person is the person whose centre is *in the world* not in the church'.[4] In a kingdom theology in which the church helps the world to understand itself 'the lay task is that of searching for, holding to, living, struggling, and dying in, *the creative centre of the culture* . . . to which we belong: it is here that the Word . . . is to be found – that is at those critical points in society where God's creativity and redemptive acts are contending with forces of meaninglessness, dispersion, disorder and despair'.[5] In such a movement participation is open to *all*. I stress the word *all* for a theology that is done in the world needs the contribution not only of Christians but of those who are *not* Christian.

Even the Church Information Office report from which I have just quoted, and which starts with so many perceptive comments, fails to follow them through and in the end proposes that lay training should start from the church. Yet this is precisely the problem. Of course we cannot do theology without the resources of Christian tradition, but we must find ways of freeing ourselves from the deformation of a theology that, because it starts from the church, never gets beyond the church.

It was over the issue of the contribution of lay people to theology that I clashed most often and most fundamentally with those who controlled church policies in the North East. The task I set myself – a task that still cries out to be done – was to release theology from the 'experts' and to develop *all* the potential theological resources of the region. In tackling this task I faced the following questions:

How to help 'ordinary' people see that theology is for them?
How to get the co-operation of academic theologians?
How to enable clergy and laity to work together appropriately?
and a question that relates to all the above questions:
How to go beyond sporadic efforts and establish a long term policy of theological development?

Though these appear to be questions of method they involve the basic content of theology – the nature of God and his purpose in the world. To tackle these questions requires a number of related activities. I realized that my aims would not be achieved quickly and therefore attempted to link each activity into longer term policies. Some of these activities, the policies we tried to develop and what was learnt in the process are described in the following case studies:

1. A lay group and a policy proposal.
2. An academic group and a policy proposal.
3. A clergy/lay group and a policy from below.

1. A lay group and a policy proposal

When I arrived in the region I was asked to act as tutor to a Sunday morning lay group that had been meeting in Stockton for several years. The members were people who through the work of the Teesside Industrial Mission had sensed that after all, in spite of negative earlier experiences, Christian faith might have relevance to their lives. Their feelings about the church and Christian faith were typical of those of many other lay people. It seemed to them that while lay people are becoming more educated in every aspect of life except that which directly concerns their faith, theology is becoming more and more rarefied and out of touch with life. They did not want to be passive recipients of the 'church's teaching', but felt that out of their experience they themselves had something to contribute. They saw the church's teaching as a set of rigid beliefs concerning which critical questioning was forbidden. This left no room for discovering a relation between Christian faith and the contemporary world. Faith was a thing apart and the church offered a 'package' to be accepted or rejected as a whole.

The theological approach I adopted in this and other groups was that which J. L. Segundo calls 'the hermeneutic circle'.[6] The hermeneutic circle is a process of reflection that begins (i) with the questions that emerge out of the participants' experience of life and then proceeds systematically through a series of steps: (ii) questioning the assumptions upon which members interpret their experiences, (iii) seeing these experiences in a wider secular context and in the light of various secular interpretations, (iv) reflecting on these experiences in the light of members' present understandings of Christian faith, (v) questioning these understandings by looking again at what is given in Bible and tradition, (vi) arriving at new understandings of Christian faith, which (vii) open up new options for response in life. Finally (viii) returning to the beginning of the circle to put these new insights to the test in life. This is a continuous process in which theology, by being closely related to daily living, is given its proper role. Segundo emphasizes two points. First, that the questions discussed must relate to fundamental issues of life and death and be sufficiently important to go beyond intellectual curiosity and demand real commitment. Secondly, we must not short-circuit or get stuck at a particular point, but must complete the circle.

Diagram 4

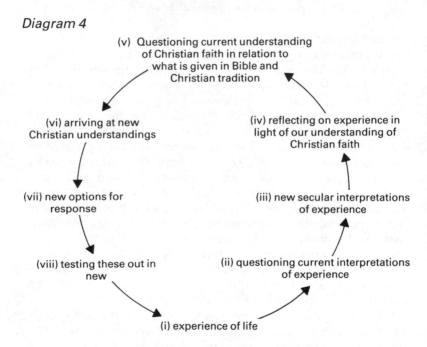

(v) Questioning current understanding of Christian faith in relation to what is given in Bible and Christian tradition

(vi) arriving at new Christian understandings

(iv) reflecting on experience in light of our understanding of Christian faith

(vii) new options for response

(iii) new secular interpretations of experience

(viii) testing these out in new

(ii) questioning current interpretations of experience

(i) experience of life

The questions the group brought from their experience concerned: the effects of organizational and technological change in industry, issues of individual and group responsibility and the value of daily work. That these were matters of vital and practical concern was not in doubt and members had plenty to say about them.

But to consider these matters in relation to what is given in Christian faith raised problems. My approach to the Bible, understandably in view of their past experience, aroused heated resistance: 'What's special about the Bible?' 'Throw it out of the window!' It was only when we had returned to the human issues, looking at them through modern literature and the insights of other faiths, that we were able to return more constructively to the Bible.

Members reluctance to study the Bible arose from the fact that in the oppressive process of socialization in society and church the Bible has been a main instrument. The God who is thus presented, far from being a liberator is an inhibitor of humanity, who in his Almightiness is unsympathetic to the realities of what is involved in being human.

The God to whom they could respond was, in contrast, one who understood and felt with humanity in its strengths, rebelliousness and weaknesses. Hence their interest in modern literature, and for some an empathy with the notion of a suffering God. I remember, for instance, one member saying from the depths of his own personal experience 'I now understand something about crucifixion'. (I noted incidentally that he did not respond when someone suggested that he should take on board the doctrine of resurrection. He was not in the 'package' business!) For these people the God they needed was one who could penetrate their inmost depths and, though few would have put it this way, one with whom they could enter into communion. I am not claiming that membership of the group met this need, but neither did their experiences in local churches, where too often prayer and worship struck them as being formal, unimaginative and unable to touch them deeply. The fact that some were looking for an appropriate spirituality was evidenced by an interest in Eastern religions.

For each member theology was not only an intellectual but a spiritual search. Much theological enquiry is a necessary clearing away of obstacles to the recognition of God. There comes for some people a moment when 'the penny drops' and that person comes alive to the reality of God. At that moment they need help in order to make an appropriate response, and it is at that moment that too often the right kind of help is not offered. This point was illustrated for me in the following way.

A member of the group who had been quite antagonistic to 'organized religion' told me that he wanted to be confirmed. As he already knew and liked one of the local vicars, there was no problem in arranging for his preparation and introduction to congregational life. To some people confirmation in these circumstances may sound like a happy ending. But this is as much a myth as to say 'they married and lived happily ever after'. In due course the man was confirmed and drawn into the life of the congregation. He became a member of the church council, a leading light on several committees, and, more constructively, he helped with the next adult confirmation class. However, his attendance at church became less and less frequent until it ceased, while his role in the confirmation class came to be considered too abrasive. He discovered other occupations that were more stretching and satisfying to him and he was not seen at church any more. Not all the fault lay with the church, but there is a depth in this man that for a moment had been stirred. Instead of being fostered this new life was smothered at birth.

The church's present lay-training programme is a sporadic and ad hoc matter. If the theological resources that were being discovered in the Sunday morning and other groups with which I was involved, were to be developed a long-term policy was required. I looked for opportunities to put this conviction into practice.

One such opportunity occurred in 1972 when I wrote a paper on Laity Education and was invited to present it to the Durham Diocesan Bishop's Council and Standing Committee. I would of course have preferred to do this in an ecumenical context, but I had to start where I could. At the time change in Durham Diocese seemed possible as discussions were then taking place about the appointment of a full-time Adult Education Officer.

In my paper I made the following points:

Every aspect of the church's work is to some extent concerned with laity education either formally or informally. Laity education cannot therefore be seen as a distinct department of the church's work, but requires all sorts of co-operations.

A lot of work of varying quality is already going on. The church should build on this rather than start new programmes.

There are two views about the purpose of the church. Is it to save people *out* of the world or to save the world? The latter requires that lay people are equipped theologically for their ministry in the world. There are two starting points for laity education – from outside the church and from inside the church. In some detail I pointed out the differences between these two approaches – in the people involved, in the method, the theological content and the educational skills needed.

Looking at what is already happening in the Diocese it is possible to see the potential for a new approach to laity education that would operate on these conclusions. Many resources are being ignored or by-passed and there is over-lapping and duplication of effort. It is a matter of using the resources already available, enabling co-operations and building up supporting services.

The church has already appointed ministers to work in some of the main areas of life: education, leisure and the arts, local neighbourhoods, to special needs and areas of special need, civic affairs and industry and commerce. Though there is only a token ministry in some cases it is at least there. In addition there are potentially supporting services for the whole enterprise in the form of education and training (education team) and research and development (theological consultancy).

My recommendations are:

to build on what is already going on,
to increase consultation across the board,
to use stimuli and insights provided by work started *outside* the
    church to enable changes to take place in the church,
to make long-term plans for the development of supporting
    services, noting the varied skills needed to put these
    proposals into effect.

At the meeting of the Bishop's Council I was given an hour before lunch in which to present the paper. The item before mine must have been controversial for when I arrived the atmosphere was far from friendly and it did not improve. Members had already received my paper and I gave a brief summary of its contents with a diagram illustrating the church in its relations with the world and the dynamics of activating the laity. As soon as I had finished speaking a senior clergyman jumped up saying 'What is *new* about this? . . . I have been doing this for years'. Then quibbles followed on the way I had expressed myself – the diagram I had drawn was wrong etc. A lay man tried to give me support but what he said was lost as the first clergyman repeated what he had already said. This was my first meeting with the Bishop's Council and I got increasingly uncomfortable. When it came to lunch time I longed to escape and felt that the last thing I wanted to do was to sit at table with these people. There were individuals who on their own would have listened to me sympathetically, but together they were at one in preventing action. This can partly be attributed to the specific nature of synodical structures. In the Bishop's Council, for instance, lay members change every few years, but the senior clergy are there *ex officio* and this may mean *ad infinitum*! Understandably many of them have acquired a certain cynicism about the possibility or desirability of change in the church. But they did not really listen, and inasmuch as they did listen, they did not hear what I said. Their aim was not to help but to criticize; not to say 'How can this help us?' but 'What is there in it with which I can disagree?' Because the church thinks in institutional terms they were also probably saying 'Who is *she* anyway?'

The man who said he had heard it all before had probably read similar points made by J. H. Oldham in the 1950s and Mark Gibbs and Ralph Morton in the 1960s. But whatever had been written or read had not changed their *practice* or the assumptions upon which that practice was based. Insofar as there had been changes they were still based on the old assumptions. My aim was not to say something new, or to get token responses, but to change the assumptions, policy and practice of the church. With regard to the possibility that anything new might happen it seemed that these people had simply ceased to believe.

I had found working with the lay groups exciting for it had revealed the richness of the theological resources that exist in lay people. The church, that so often complains about its lack of resources, should, I thought, want to make the most of such 'frozen assets'. But my attempts to suggest ways of opening up these resources was met by the church's institutional resistance to change. We need to reflect on this experience, which in different forms was repeated for me many times.

2. An academic group and a policy proposal

Academic theologians are essential to theology but their work is only part of the theological task. From the point of view of a theology that is seen as a system of academically acquired knowledge, a theological heirarchy is assumed, in which academic theologians, 'the experts', are at the top, clergy are in the middle as filters or censors, and lay people are passive recipients of whatever manages to get through.

In contrast theology that is seen as reflection on life in the light of Christian faith, requires data not only from past Christian tradition but from present experience of life, including experience of God. This should be supplied by all groups. In such co-operation all have something to give and all have something to

Theology for Everyone

gain. The 'field-workers', that is the clergy and lay people, gain from seeing their experience and insights in the perspective of a disciplined understanding of Christian tradition. Academic theologians gain by having opportunity to give greater weight to the realities of daily life. In order to get a co-operative process going, a conversation between the three groups is required.

In my first year I made contacts with academic theologians at Durham and Newcastle Universities, Ushaw and Cranmer theological colleges and the Polytechnics and Colleges of Education in the region. In September 1970 I invited a mixed group of academic theologians, clergy and lay people to explore the possibilities of co-operation, by meeting together over a period, which in the event led to bi-monthly meetings being held during the next five years.

Our method was to alternate between starting meetings from a practical situation in order to discover in discussion what theological points might be relevant to it, and from a Christian doctrine in order to discover whether it had practical implications for daily living. At our first meeting we asked a lay man to introduce a discussion of his situation. He was a personnel manager in a large engineering works and described how he had to train young people for 'boring and frustrating jobs' trying to help them find some satisfaction. In the discussion we asked the following questions:

Do we understand the relevant facts and factors of the actual situation?
Are there any theological points which would help us:
(i) to understand the situation from a theological point of view?
(ii) to make some sort of Christian judgment on the situation?
Is there anything a Christian can say which would help people who have to make a response to the situation and wish to do so in a Christian manner?

The reaction of the academic theologians was to focus sharply on the biblical reference to work. They pointed out the dual understanding of work that runs through the Old Testament and throughout Christian history:

(i) The necessity of work resulting from the fall; work as a burden and a curse.
(ii) Work as participation in creation and redemption.

Other members of the group pointed out that Christian faith is concerned with large underlying themes and has little to say about work, especially work in an industrial society. To isolate work and to expect to find satisfaction in it is artificial and wrong. The question of job satisfaction might be approached better by asking: Where do I find value as a person? What makes sense of both the positive and negative aspect of what I do in life? The particular judgment we make on the situation depends on our general view of life and of the nature of man and society. This is largely shaped by factors other than Christian belief. Whatever action may be possible will be more than the response of one individual but should lead to political action aimed at changing society.

In spite of our declared aim of discovering what a Christian might say to help response to the situation, the discussion took off from the reality that had been presented. The speaker, who had come with the expectation that he would receive help, felt in the end that members were not concerned with *his* problem.

Subsequently we devoted two meetings to different approaches to the doctrine of creation. The first of these meetings started from a presentation of the biblical doctrine which, it was pointed out, is primarily about God, though people today are seizing on it as a peg upon which to hang their concern about ecology. This misses the point, the presenter said, for the need is not that people should take the world seriously but that they should take God seriously. The second presentation started from the point of relevance and suggested that creation is about people coming into being and that the doctrine's relevance is to be found in people's struggle for individuality.

These and other meetings revealed deep divergences within the group about the nature and practice of theology. Most of the lay people were out of their depth and our search for lay people to share in the discussions underlined the lack of adequate lay development in the churches. The clergy found the group useful as for them the attempt to think theologically about life is a daily concern. For the academics the meetings were a demand on their time and they did not really see the point of the exercise. Their main concerns were professional and they had little time for the unformulated issues of daily life and for what seemed to them, inconsequential discussion. They wanted to *help* but they did not see that they themselves stood to gain anything.

Fortunately my objective of working with academic theologians was also a concern of the Bishop of Durham and his interest led to a definite policy proposal.

The Bishop had visited the 'mixed' group and seen the possibility of broadening its scope. In December 1971 he hosted a consultation in his rooms at Durham Castle, describing the purpose in this way:

> Discussion will centre on problems which arise when the teaching of theology is considered in relation to a practical ministry. It is clear that many people in a Christian ministry today often need help in relating their academic studies to the actual situations they meet, and I am anxious to discover whether, and if so what, more can be done, and by whom, and when, to help students and others to acquire an approach to theological study that will enable them to relate what so often is separated. In this context, I would greatly value the opportunity of an informal discussion with members of the Faculty of Theology of the University of Durham, and others who are specially concerned with education and with training for Christian ministry.

I had prepared a paper for a consultation on 'Dogmatic or Contextual Theology' held by the World Council of Churches in Bossey during the summer of 1971 and this was used as background to our discussions at the Castle ('Secular Experience and Theological Thinking' – see Appendix). I was thankful that I only had to play a small part during the actual meeting. The Bishop led the discussion, passionately defending the need for a new orientation of theology. It seemed that few people really understood the radical changes he was advocating or if they did understand they resisted following through its implications for their own practice of theology. Persistently they talked as if what was under discussion was a matter of the *application* rather than the *substance* of theological truth. Fears emerged that the academic quality of theology was being threatened. Defensively they said 'Students do relate theology and life for they too read the papers and live in communities'.

The head of Department spoke for the others saying 'The Department will *help* when asked, but of course we have our own job to do'. In the face of this refusal to comprehend it was difficult for those who felt that something more was at stake to lead the discussion in more positive directions. Two members had been particularly helpful to me from the time I came to the North East. One, who was a lecturer at the University as well as being a tutor at Ushaw College threw out a life-line suggesting that what was needed was a University backed Ecumenical Pastoral Institute. The proposal was taken up with relief by those who were feeling uncomfortable with the negative tone of the discussion. They asked me to work with the proposer to prepare a draft outline for a Pastoral Institute and the Bishop undertook to chair a small working group to carry the proposals forward.

In March 1973 my colleague and I presented our proposals to the working group which had been enlarged and included among others the Roman Catholic Bishop of Hexham and Newcastle. In view of later developments (including the establishment in 1981 of the North of England Institute for Christian Education) it is worth recording the outline of our plans:

A Durham Ecumenical Pastoral Institute should be sponsored by the Faculty of Theology of the University of Durham. Its purpose would be to assist the work of the church in the world by studying in an inter-disciplinary manner key issues of the world and furthering actual responses and possible future responses of the church in society. Participants would be lay and ordained persons with experience in church and/or society who after a two-year part-time course would be awarded a diploma by written examination and a project.

It was soon after this meeting that, with the Bishop's first heart attack, things began to go wrong. The tragedy of the Bishop's illness and death cannot be told here. Among those who had been influenced by him many hopes were quenched and in my work there were far reaching effects. Planning for the Durham Ecumenical Pastoral Institute continued and the Committee was chaired by a member of the Theology Department of Durham University. I suffered further losses when two of my main supporters moved away to other jobs. Those who remained on the Committee were unable to maintain Ian Ramsey's vision.

In an attempt to awaken vision I produced a paper advocating something on the lines of the German Academies (without their lavish buildings):

The Academies were founded in order to overcome the inner division in people, which relegates Christian faith to the private department of life. They aim to make a contribution to a Christian understanding of the issues of social change in a way that goes beyond the possibilities of the resources of any local congregation or denomination. Their educational style is:

(i) To start with questions of life.

(ii) To bring together cross-sections of those who share a common concern or responsibility. These may be Christian or non-Christian, of any denomination or none, clergy or lay.

(iii) To regard those who come not as pupils but as contributors from their own experience and helpers of each other.

(iv) To work in a secular style in which the Christian message is passed on as a contribution integral to the issue discussed and the Gospel is discussed as frankly as anything else.[7]

I appended to the paper an analysis of the many exciting things going on in the North East in the form of clergy training, lay training, involvement in social issues and specific sectors of life such as industry, politics and the arts. In all these enterprises there were elements of training. The purpose of the Institute would be to bring together and strengthen this training in a co-ordinated policy. The committee however knew nothing about these activities and their objections showed a lack of comprehension of or empathy with my approach. They asked: 'Can clergy and laity work together?' 'How can academic standards be safeguarded?' Inevitably there was an attempt to show that the work was already being done or about to be done, in this case in a Diploma of Pastoral Studies put forward by Cranmer College that had just got through the University's Board. Plans for the Institute were changed and modified until their original purpose was entirely obscured. The Committee wanted the University to have control, but their fear of lowering academic standards made them want to distance it in some way. They suggested that it should come under the Extra-Mural Department, in which some of them had led courses. Eventually they suggested that instead of starting with a two-year diploma there should be a pilot course of ten evenings!

There was clearly no future in this kind of proposal. I was glad when Bishop Habgood arrived and I was able to recommend to him that the proposal be shelved. I did not want to foster a no-change institute.

This was only one of the pieces of work I did with academic theologians. Many of the clergy and lay people I worked with were struggling to respond to their situation with inadequate theological backing. I constantly pressed the Industrial Mission Association to set up means by which chaplains and others might reflect on their experience theologically under the discipline of academic supervision. This led to my involvement in the early stages of the courses currently being run by William Temple Foundation with Manchester University and by Hull University.[8] With Ian Ramsey's help I visited people in other parts of the country who shared my concern and am now in touch with a national and to a lesser extent international network of theological resources.

My conclusion is that only some academic theologians are able to work with others around the issues of life. Yet it is crucial that there should be such people. Creative theology, from the Exodus to the Holocaust has always been a response to what is happening in the world. If we believe in the God whose word came to Moses in the desert, we need to know what God's word is to us today. In this search there is only a part, but a necessary part for the academic theologian.

The group that reviewed my work as theological consultant criticized my lack of contact with academic theologians: 'We are anxious' they said 'that there should be closer links with the universities in the region than has been the case hitherto.' My answer to this is 'Yes, but only if this is a two-way relationship'.

3. A lay/clergy group and a policy from below

I set out my strategy in one of my first reports, and outlined it again in *Theology in an Industrial Society*. Central to it was the aim to build up a team of theologians clerical and lay who would be the spearhead of a systematic development and use of the potential theological resources throughout the region.

The setting up of the Theological Development Group in September 1975 aimed to implement this manifesto and was to be the first step in the creation of what I termed a Theological Agency. This would consist of a core-group servicing a wide network of people who would be involved in one way or another with the theological process. What I had in mind was quite different from the centralized, professional practice of theology that is current in the churches. I wanted to create an organic network that could stimulate and support theological reflection throughout both church and world. Some sort of organization would be needed, but it would be different from that which at present existed. I had already discovered that this would be a threat to those who had invested in the old order, for if it was successful it would demand a re-direction of the current training arrangements of the churches. I saw that this would be a long task and that it was important to ensure that questions of structure should follow rather than precede those of vision. For the pilot group I therefore chose people who shared my vision. I invited six clergy and four lay people who from my contacts had emerged as being most committed to the search for connections between Christian faith and daily living. Apart from the fact that I was the only woman, the group represented a reasonable cross-section of interests and a regional, ecumenical spread.

We reckoned that the identification of our own theological needs would to some extent indicate the nature of the needs of others. We therefore spent a good deal of time analysing our own situations, our struggles to understand and communicate the gospel, our successes and our failures.

We began by each filling in a simple questionaire describing the possibilities and difficulties we were encountering in one specific situation where we were trying to relate faith and life. The situations included:

a layman taking part in a house group
a lecturer in his membership of a curriculum committee
a parish priest in his leadership of the congregation
an industrial chaplain in his membership of a management/ union consultative committee
a shop steward trying to share his faith with his fellow workers
a team rector building up a congregation in a new town
a personnel manager working with industrial mission in his works.

Following the method described in my first example (hermeneutic circle), we spent the first year working through each person's story. As these were real situations, members were able to say whether what was said at the meetings made any difference to what actually happened.

Summarizing what came out of this detailed exploration we shared our dreams of the kind of supportive structures that might sustain us and others in our search. A variety of models was proposed including an 'Iona for the North East',[9] not a place so much as an instrument for the development of spiritual life: and a model that gave exclusive emphasis to the relation of Christian faith to the social issues of the region. I wanted something that while including both these things, could not be put in a separate compartment, but would re-orientate theological practice as a whole. My notes for this particular meeting summarize the kind of theology with which I am concerned and which is the subject of this book:

The need is for a theology of a specific kind. It is:
related to life as it is experienced today;
enables people to explore the resources of Christian tradition as they bear on their actual situations. (In the face of misunderstandings about theologies that start from life, I must emphasise that the theology with which I am concerned draws upon *all* the resources of Christian tradition.)
collaborative, engaging all sorts of people lay and clerical;
inter-active in that it is not purely cerebral but has a place within the totality of living – prayer, worship, dynamics of fellowship and authority, passion, endurance, suffering and action.

The Theological Agency would not be a training institute but would further the development and appropriate use of all sorts of persons who in all sorts of ways could help people *where they are* to engage in this kind of theological reflection.

The plan was not to develop people's theological skills and then inject them into existing groups, so much as to help people do better what they were already trying to do. For instance such people would include two men from the Sunday morning group who had started groups in their own homes, the shop steward who was trying to share his faith with his workmates, the clergyman developing collaborative ministry in his parish, others who in a variety of situations were involved with others in trying to make sense of their situation. In short our aim was to get theology going where it is needed among all sorts of people engaged in all aspects of life.

We realized that at present there was little understanding or support for a Theological Agency and concluded that

at this stage the agency should exist primarily as a resource for the work of the theological consultant and that she would be the person through whom the churches would at present operate. . . . In this 'hidden' period the agency would have to create its own organization in a style and shape that would be as it wished it to be when it does go public, and it would have to get on with the job by laying sound foundations of work.[10]

In this group, and throughout the project, clergy and laity worked together. While each contributed, from their own different experience, knowledge and abilities, there was no stereotyping by role, and the laity did not feel impelled to defer to the clergy. This represented a model of what '*laos*' – the church should be.

Members showed a wonderful commitment to the task and it was unusual for anyone to miss a meeting. We were to begin with a small enough group to work together easily, but we had to take the risk of opening up to a wider constituency. In February 1978 we therefore embarked on a new stage of exploration by inviting nineteen new members to join the original group. We were asking for their help in sharpening the theological issues and carrying forward the task of setting up a theological agency, but we only wanted them to join us if they felt that membership would contribute something to their own work and concerns. We were able in the new members to redress the male/female imbalance and, by following the first group's policy of recruiting in three main parts of the region, we were able to do most of the work in sub-groups held in Newcastle, Sunderland and Cleveland under the leadership of members of the original group. Each sub-group developed in its own way, thus making their specific contributions to the aim of broadening our understanding of the nature of theology. The Newcastle group was especially concerned with its internal dynamics, the Sunderland group struggled with dimensions of spirituality. The Cleveland group tried to develop skills that would make it possible for members to become enablers in other groups. Even after four years' work there was a long way to go if this approach was to be effective. I felt however, that together we were developing a way of structuring the theological task that could give the sustained support to laity and clergy that would enable their faith to make an impact on the world.

Before we could go further we had to come to terms with the reality of our situation in relation to the institutions of the church. Policy making from below can only progress so far. In our final joint review session progress towards the creation of a Theological Agency came to a temporary (?) halt, when members pointed out that the efficacy of such an Agency depended on clarification of the role of the theological consultant. It was this that finally decided me to set up a group to review the work of the Consultancy.

If the Theological Consultancy was to continue – and I could not go on for ever – it must have some acceptance by the church *qua* institution. I had made the Theological Agency the focus of my strategy so it was right that the whole question of the role of the consultant should arise in that setting.

There were crucial differences between (a) current assumptions in the educational work of the church and (b) what was proposed in the Theological Agency:

> the aim is in (a) to build up the church, in (b) to infect the world;
>
> the full-time agents in (a) operate from the centre, in (b) they build up a network within which to work in the world;
>
> the agents in (a) perform a teaching role, in (b) they are enablers drawing out and using the skills of others;
>
> the movement in (a) is one-way in which people come to the 'experts' in order to learn, in (b) is outward into the world, and between those involved there is a two-way movement in which all are learners and all teachers and in which church and world learn from each other.

My vision is of God as he is to be known in life. Getting theology going is to me a process of enabling people where they are to recognize and respond to God. The Theological Agency was to be a main structure by which this was done. It would be a flexible, organic growth supported by a strong backbone – the core group. Planned change would be built into this group to avoid dangers of rigidity. The theological consultant would service the operation and ensure continuity.

I was aware that this vision conflicted with current assumptions and that if it succeeded it would subvert present structures.

Institutions have their own ways of dealing with what threatens them. The crudest and last resort is open opposition. In the case of a weak threat institutions can simply freeze them out. If however, the threat is too strong to be ignored, the next stratagem is to embrace it, draw it into the institution's own orbit and subtly extract its teeth! What actually happened in the case not only of the Theological Agency but of the threat the consultancy posed to the institution is described in the next chapter.

The examples I have given in this chapter show that if the

institution did not respond, people certainly did. I have only been able to give a glimpse of the excitement and overwhelming response that I experienced in my attempts to ground theology in life. For this I am profoundly thankful. There is no doubt in my mind that there are among all sorts of people many theological resources. But these remain only *potential* resources, for as far as any change in the church's approach to theology or consequent change of structure is concerned I conclude that the point has not been taken.

VIII Alternative Church Structures

A change in theology implies a change in structure. A belief that God's purpose is to redeem the world and to establish his kingdom, requires a church that can co-operate with him and that is structured for that purpose. I could not get far in my task of enabling theology to be related to life without coming into conflict with church structures. What has already been shown and what this chapter will make even clearer is that the structures defeated me every time. My only success (and that was a considerable one) was that I managed to leave a successor in the structures.

This chapter is concerned with church structures, and the fact that these should be a response to the particular situation and should in themselves express the nature of God and his concern for the world. But this is not how the church sees its task.

The church is not geared to making God known in the world, but to its own survival. Though this fact should concern us, it should not cause us to despair. If God is in history, he is also in the history of the church; if there is hope for history, there is hope for the church.

When we look at the past history of the church, even within the limits of our own region, it is clear that through the ages many changes have taken place in the way the church has structured its task and resources. Our problem today is that we are so stuck in a comparatively recent part of tradition that we imagine this is what the church always has been and always must be.

Today changes are taking place, and the question we must ask is 'Are changes being forced upon the church by outside pressures (money, manpower etc.) or are they a response to a vision of God in his relationships with the world?'

In addressing this question I use five examples from my experience as theological consultant. Each example raises a particular structural issue, but all point to confusions about church, world and kingdom and to the institutional resistance of the church to change:

1. Piecemeal adaptation to change – sector ministries
2. Change from below – *Structuring the church for Mission*
3. Managerial muddles
4. Institutional resistance to change
5. Opportunities and choices – The North of England Institute of Christian Education

1. Piecemeal adaptation to change – sector ministries

Simply to add new ministries or structures in response to newly perceived needs only leads to confusion. Instead one must ask basic questions about the purpose of the total operation: What is it for? What structure will best help to achieve that purpose?

This point is illustrated by the development of sector ministry. Traditional church structures are based on the assumption that parochial ministry geared to the building up of the church is the norm. Synodical government is constructed on representation from parishes, with the single exception of a few places on General Synod for the universities. A lack of understanding and commitment to the church's responsibilities in the world has led to any other form of ministry being defined negatively as 'non-parochial'. Bishop Ramsey's belief that the church must minister to the world and that in order to do that it must minister ecumenically, led to a rapid development of sector ministry in the Diocese of Durham and inevitably to organizational problems. In 1970 he therefore invited representatives of sector ministry to meet with him at regular intervals. A list of those who attended the first meeting (which only included 'heads of departments'), indicates the scope of sector ministry in the Diocese at that time: Chaplain to Arts and Recreation, Hospital Chaplains, Industrial Mission Chaplains (Teesside and Northumbria), Social Responsibility Officers (Durham and Teesside), Family Welfare representative, Stewardship Officer, Theological Consultant, Director of Education, Director of Further Training (Clergy). This is not an exhaustive list of those who might be termed 'sector ministers' but it is enough to demonstrate the nature of the issue.

Although all these people were lumped together as 'sector ministers' there were several basic differences that made it difficult for anything to be achieved. First of all they represented two different types of responsibility: those who operate within a particular 'sector' such as industry, the arts, hospitals, and those who offer a 'specialist' service across the board such as education and training, and theological consultancy.

Secondly there are the established (establishment) ministries and those which have been newly created. This division sometimes, but not always, coincided with another divide – that between theological attitudes that were either traditional or radical. The Board of Education for instance, which has statutory backing in its concern for church schools had not broken out of its didactic theological mould. Hospital chaplains along with prison chaplains, which have strong establishment support from the state, tend to focus on the traditional pastoral approach. But that this is not always the case was apparent to us in the fact that the hospital chaplain in this particular group took a radical approach that was directed not only to pastoral but to structural issues of the health service.

The uniting factor in the meeting was the fact that the main responsibility of all the members was non-parochial. All therefore felt excluded from the structures of the church and unable to make their contribution to its mission policy.

There was no easy answer to the question of structure. Ministries that deal directly with issues of society must relate primarily to the structures of society rather than to those of the church, and moreover the fact that they operate ecumenically adds to the complexity. The hospital chaplain for instance wrote: 'In my job I need to be linked to: (a) the Government Health areas, (b) the local church, (c) colleagues in other sector ministries, (d) the Deanery Synod, (e) the Council of Churches.' It was understandable that he felt that efforts to help him relate more effectively to the Diocesan structures led only to more meetings and less time in which to do his work.

There was clearly no chance of creating structures that could deal with this kind of complexity in the context of a meeting of Anglican sector ministers with an Anglican Bishop. Rather than solving the problem the meeting exacerbated it by further isolating sector ministers as a separate group. The obvious lesson is that structural issues cannot be solved piecemeal.

The Bishop, however, continued to make matters worse, by making new appointments without seeing that each new appointment had implications for those already in operation. This issue came to a head with the proposed appointment of an Adult

Education Officer. Most sector ministers are concerned with Adult Education in one way or another, and the Bishop invited discussion of the matter in the sector ministers' meeting. The sector ministers' approach to Christian education starts necessarily from the issues of the world and proceeds from this starting point to draw out the Christian significance of those issues. The aims proposed by the Director of Education were in stark contrast for they focussed primarily on the church and to a lesser extent on the educational sector:

(i) Helping the faithful to understand what it means to be a Christian.

(ii) Helping enquirers find the right questions and answers to them.

(iii) Being an effective presence in the business of education as administered by the state.

It was as part of this discussion that I was asked to prepare a paper on Laity Education which I later presented to the Bishop's Council and Standing Committee. I have described in Chapter VII the way in which any suggestion that there should be a change in the traditional pattern of adult education was brushed aside. In the end the Director of Education's job description went through unchanged, and an Adult Education Officer was appointed without any structured relationship with the educational work being done by sector ministers.

As nothing was done to solve either the problem of new appointments or the wider issue of structures, commitment to the sector ministers' meeting decreased, and no one was sorry when, on coming to the Diocese, Bishop Habgood decided to disband the group.

2. Change from below – Structuring the Church for Mission

An attempt in Teesside to relate purpose and structure picks up the issue of sector ministry and poses a question concerning the appropriate scale upon which to base a model of the church in mission.

The structural problem was particularly acute in Teesside where a lot of creative work that was being done ecumenically was hampered by the fact that the area was cut in half by both Anglican and Roman Catholic Diocesan boundaries.

In July 1969 (the date of my arrival) a booklet *Structuring the Church for Mission*[1] had just been published and I was invited to meet with the working group out of whose discussions it had come. The booklet contains a statement of aims towards the fulfilment of which a few people have worked consistently over many years – so far without success. It puts its case briefly in five short chapters:

First, it analyses the area. Teesside became a County Borough in 1968 (though in 1974 it was again sub-divided into Districts and became part of the new County of Cleveland). A report, *The Teesplan*,[2] drew attention to a need, in the secular context, to overcome 'parochialism' and develop new forms of co-operation: 'With all the tensions of parochial loyalties, the local government officials are trying to forge themselves into an efficient unit with which to grapple with large-scale problems.'

Secondly, the present position of the church in the area is described: Its sex ratio – more women than men, its social ratio – more attendance by people from private housing in the suburbs than from council housing and the inner city, more professional than working-class members, its concerns – 'It seems that most church-goers have withdrawn from the socio/political organisations in which the main decisions affecting the future of our community life are made.'

Thirdly, it looks at the Bible and suggests that vital aspects of a full theology of mission are being repressed by the churches. Their mission is primarily concerned with conversion and individual salvation to the exclusion of the church's function 'to search for the hand of God at work in the world and to be co-workers with God in his mission . . . the realisation of the full potentialities of all creation and its ultimate reconciliation and unity in Christ. That is to say the aim is to establish fullness of life, peace, love, justice, liberty, reconciliation, enabling people to be fully human. The Church's task must be seen in terms of entering into partnership with God in the present historic events and to renew society.'

Fourthly it proposes a new structure that will enable this mission to be undertaken. This comprises a Teesside Ecumenical Council of Urban Mission relating to the Teesside Council of Churches and having five areas of concern: local neighbourhood ministries, crisis ministries (covering statutory and voluntary social services), civic concerns, industry and commerce, training and research. It points out that ministers are already working in most of these areas, but that the numbers in local ministry are out of proportion in comparison with the few who work in the other four areas. One proposal is therefore for an increase in the number of 'sector ministers'. The new organization would be managed by a Board including representatives from the denominations with specialists e.g. Industrial Mission staff, Social Responsibility Officer, and a 'healthy balance of lay people'. It would be financed by the churches of Teesside. The final section aims to deal with the kind of resistance that was anticipated.

In order to begin to implement these proposals, heads of churches concerned were invited in autumn 1969 to a one-day consultation at which I was asked to give a theological introduction. I later became a member of the follow-up committee. This committee struggled on for several years until at last it ran out of steam. From time to time the idea has been revived in one form or another. Currently for instance the church leaders are supporting an effort to make a united approach to Cleveland's industrial crisis in a project known as 'Respond'.[3] The only structural change that has come about as a result of these proposals is an agreement between the two Anglican Dioceses in which the Bishop of Whitby (a suffragan of York Diocese) has been given an ill-defined responsibility within the whole of Teesside. Even this minimum adaptation seems now to have been rescinded. There are three obvious reasons why so little has been achieved.

The first reason relates to the sheer weight of the traditional structures. People would read the booklet and say 'How interesting' or, as happened to me with the Laity Education paper (see Chapter VII), 'What is *new* in this? We've heard it all before'. But they made no changes and never intended to make any, for they knew what the cost would be not only in financial terms, but in lost autonomy. A parallel may be drawn between this experience and what is happening in relationships between National and Local Government. A great deal of local experimentation is allowed and even encouraged, but in the end Government is not seriously threatened by any amount of community politics. In the same way the church's centres of power remain untouched by skirmishes at grass roots.

Secondly, in my opinion, the case was over-simplified and the case for sector ministry over-stated. The clarity of the case made was one of the strengths of the booklet, but that initial statement needed to be worked into more sensitively complex proposals. It was recognized that the church's response to a complex industrial society needs to be multi-form, but it failed to make room for different points of view. In this case the dominant proponents were sector ministers who are extremely creative people and to whom church life in Teesside owes an immense debt. Their dominance, however, led to too much stress being put on the things to which they personally were committed. Frontier groups, for instance, were presented as if they were the answer to every need. Contributions that should have been made by other people were not heard. There were for instance few positive contributions to the debate from local church ministers. Too often, instead of putting a case for the development of aspects of their work, they remained silent or reacted defensively. Vision cannot be imposed on people. Somehow or other they must be helped to *see* for themselves.

Thirdly I believed that for such radical proposals the scale was wrong and that a Regional rather than a sub-regional change was more likely to be effective. I had sound reasons for this belief:

The North-East Region has a natural identity geographically, historically and culturally.

The region has been given statutory recognition within the Government Regional structure. Although the Northern Region includes Cumbria the regional offices are in Newcastle.

Within this identity there is considerable diversity which enriches the situation and counteracts tendencies to over-simplification or over-'parochialism'.

There are varied resources within the region including the Universities of Durham and Newcastle and the theological resources of the Universities and the theological colleges.

The churches have taken first steps towards adapting their work to a regional pattern in, for instance, the North-East Ecumenical Group – and a point that was obviously decisive for me – in my own appointment.

My own aim was from the start to develop a Regional, Ecumenical pattern of work and structure to match (see Chapter I).

3. *Managerial muddles*

To work on large scale regional, ecumenical lines inevitably raises questions of management style. It is this issue that I now address.

In thinking regionally and ecumenically I was following the pattern laid down by Bishop Ramsey and the terms of my own appointment. Before my arrival Bishop Ramsey had discussed my job with the North-East Ecumenical Group (NEEG). As this was the only ecumenical structure covering the area in which I was to work I saw the NEEG as the logical structure to which I should relate. I was soon made to realize, however, that the NEEG felt they had no responsibility for me or my work. I found that it was I who had to take the first initiative in making contact with them, and in order to do so I approached them with specific requests, for instance for nominations to or reporting on two ecumenical study groups, or to report on the Tyne and Wear Urban Ministry courses (see Chapter V). On these occasions members of NEEG made me feel that they were helping me. That I might have been able to help them never crossed their minds.

Although NEEG claimed to be a non-executive body, they were an extremely powerful forum to which church leaders of the region were committed and through which backing was given to a number of ecumenical projects.

One such project was, for example, 'Action North East'. In 1972 the Archbishop of York asked church leaders throughout the North to support him in a 'Call to the North' which would inaugurate an intensive period of ecumenical mission. Bishop Ramsey decided that in the North East such a mission should lay special stress on action, so under the auspices of NEEG he launched 'Action North East'. The initial announcement stated that a programme would continue until at least 1975 with the aim of helping Christians 'to a deeper understanding of their faith and its bearing upon the questions of everday life . . . local initiative will be the starting point as local groups decide what it is they wish to study with a view to undertaking action within the community at large'.

Here was a point at which I might have helped. But, although this was very much within my area of concern, I had to respond to these plans as they were made public. Quite apart from the fact that I had already spent several years identifying issues and resources in the region, I felt that as theological consultant I should be involved at the planning stage of such projects. This was not a matter of my muscling in on something simply because I was interested. I was *employed* and *paid* for this very purpose. If the 'powers' that be did not think I was up to the job, they should have sacked me. To go on employing me while at the same time actively stopping me from doing the job was an amazing abdication of responsibility.

Bishop Ramsey did in fact tell me when the project was launched that he hoped that 'Action North East' would help to develop new ecumenical structures and that he wished me to play a part in this, but before he had time to clarify his thinking on this matter he was taken ill. The project continued to be co-ordinated by a regional team, who were at pains to point out that their approach would be non-directional. Initiative would lie with the councils of churches and other local groups while the regional team would give support in various ways. Though the project continued for a couple more years it missed the Bishop's driving force and petered out.

Issues of management style run throughout this story. In my experience the church seems unaware of managerial styles other than those that are authoritarian or *laissez-faire*. In all churches the power of individuals has been modified by bureaucratic structures which give a semblance of shared control.

In spite of Synodical Government Bishops of the Church of England maintain a good deal of power to 'work the system', but not enough to implement decisive policy. The clash between the old hierarchical style and the new bureaucratic style leaves uncertainty about who exercises power. It is easiest to take the line of least resistance so that no one takes responsibility.

The same problem affects every institution, and though none have a completely satisfactory answer much has been learnt for instance by industry about responsible, participative management. For this to be effective a great deal of skill and time is needed as people work together to clarify aims, set short and long term objectives and monitor progress. But the church ignores such skills and, if it cannot have a simple answer concludes that there is no alternative but to 'leave it to the Holy Spirit'.

The style of management Christians adopt depends on what they believe about God and about people. Structure and belief should not be separated. In my own practice for instance, in the projects described in this chapter I tried to use an 'enabling' style. An enabling model is based on the belief that God is at work in the world and in people. It is not we who initiate mission but God who calls us to work with him. No project is in itself the beginning of an operation, for we act within situations in which many things positive and negative, are already happening. God, and other people, are there before us. This means we have to be sensitive to what is already happening. If things are to be carried forward, management is still needed. It is in the light of a specific vision that what is significant is identified. Objectives and a time-table have to be agreed and what happens monitored against these goals. Plans cannot just be left to the inspiration of the moment. People need information and time to think things through so that they come to meetings with their own ideas and proposals. In this way there can be real sharing including shared leadership. To have the kind of serving, enabling role that I had in many projects is not to be devoid of ideas oneself. My ideas were creative of what happened, but if they had had no echo in the people with whom I worked nothing would have happened. In some way one must articulate the aspirations, however unconscious, of others in such a way that they recognize and accept them as their own.

The success of Mao Tse Tung was that in the end people said 'We did it ourselves'. Such a statement emerges from a style of leadership that, far from being *laissez-faire*, revolutionizes people's way of seeing things, creates a sense of newness and thereby the possibility of real change. Ian Ramsey had this style and ability. He made people feel that what they were doing mattered, and at the same time that they should and could achieve much more. Those who glimpse such a vision need a lot of sustaining. They should not be left to stand alone. Someone has to clarify medium as well as long-term tasks, help them to develop skills, find local allies and new ways of working together. This does not just happen, it has to be planned and managed.

Those people who from time to time suggested that I was trying to cover too large an area were assuming a model in which the 'leader' does everything him/herself or is the hub around which all activities revolve. My model was different for I aimed to release other people's resources so that they could exercise leadership in their own right. In many of the projects with which I was concerned, such as the Tyne and Wear and the theological college courses, I took steps to build up teams of people who could carry the work forward without me.

In this example I have focussed on the management of large scale operations but the issue of management style is not only relevant to regional operations. In fact it is the paternalistic/ authoritarian model that operates at parish level that influences management style throughout the church. If at the parish level there is little comprehension of what it is to work with people, so

that, for instance, teams are often teams only in name, this will be
the case at other levels. To consider working regionally and
ecumenically means stepping right outside 'normal' practice. My
next example shows how strong is the pull that drags us back into
traditional patterns.

4. Institutional resistance to change

In 1973, following the death of Ian Ramsey, John Habgood
became Bishop of Durham. He quickly realized that he had to do
something about the structural confusion and in 1975 put a re-
organization of the Diocese into effect.

From the point of view of my own job I was also considering the
matter of structure. I felt that some of the set-backs I experienced
might be due to the fact that people had not had the chance to
share the vision upon which my work was based. In order to get
through this blockage I wrote my first book, *Theology in an
Industrial Society*. This set out the beliefs and strategy upon which
I was operating, and had an obvious bearing on the structures of
the church. I made the final chapters as sharp and precise as
possible for I saw them as a manifesto and hoped it would be
sufficiently convincing to lead to shared action. I was encouraged
in this view when Bishop John brought his advance copy to a
Diocesan meeting and holding it up said 'Here is the mission
policy we need!'

My optimism was however short lived. The Bishop's main
concern at the time was the introduction of the new Diocesan
structure. This was an attempt to tidy things up and he wanted to
fit me in somewhere. It was only a week or two after the meeting
just mentioned that he asked me to become secretary of the newly
formed Diocesan Social Responsibility Committee. This invitation was a revelation to me of how little he had understood what I
had written. It was an agonizing decision for me to make. I knew
that he wanted to help me to make a contribution to the Diocese,
but I felt that to try to do this through any Diocesan Committee
would only confuse the purpose of my job. I looked at the matter
from all angles and discussed it with my Advisory Group. In the
end, in spite of the obvious risk, I decided to do the job for a
limited time if only as a matter of 'obedience'. In addition to the
Social Responsibility Committee the Bishop made me a member
of other committees to which he saw my work relating – logically

this meant *all* the committees. As my role on these committees was not defined this led not only to a lot of work, but also to a lot of frustration. I look back to that date as a watershed, a point at which I gave up hope.

How could I possibly develop a network of theological resources and get theology flowing throughout the whole organization, if I had to spend my time in all these meetings and if there was confusion about my role. If I was secretary of one committee how could I avoid being identified with one part of the church's work?

My despair was not only caused by what happened in Durham Diocese. The Bishop of Newcastle (R. O. Bowlby) had also had an advance copy of my book. Knowing him as I did, I hoped for some encouragement. But again my hopes were dashed. The Bishop saw my book as an occasion for exercising his episcopal function of defending the faith. In a blistering review article in the Diocesan paper he asked 'What is this but the Social Gospel of fifty years ago?'[4] He did not see that I was raising issues about specific things to do with his own Diocese, or that it had implications for my future relationship with the Diocese.

I did not give up hope in what I was doing, for I had too many positive proofs of the possibilities it contained.

I did not give up hope in God, in fact just the opposite for I was cast more than ever on his resources rather than my own. I was confirmed in my belief that though nothing we do is wasted, it is God who brings the kingdom. But I did give up hope in the possibility of change in the church's structures by which I felt compromised and trapped.

There are of course different ways of responding to this kind of experience. Many people will say 'Why did she not get out if things were so hopeless?' That suggestion was in fact made to me by one of the Theological Consultancy Review group. When it seemed that it might not be possible to get another Theological Consultant appointed, he suggested that I set up a trust and worked from outside the church. My answer to such proposals is that in spite of all that is wrong with the church I see it as an essential vehicle for the continuing transmission of the gospel. No doubt some people should loosen their links with the church. Others, and I feel that this includes me, must, through their involvement *in* the church continue to challenge the church to assume its proper character and responsibilities.

5. *Opportunities and choices – The North of England Institute of Christian Education (NEICE)*

While I was working from below at a regional ecumenical policy, other moves were taking place at the top.

In February 1977 a paper, *Theological Training: A Policy for the Future*,[5] was presented to the Anglican General Synod. Its main proposal was that theological training of all kinds (clergy and laity) should take place in a limited number of Regional Institutes. These would be formed around the main centres of theological resources where there were university and theological colleges. The Archbishop of Canterbury[6] had written to the Bishop of Durham asking him to explore the possibility of establishing such a centre in the North East. At the same time the merging of the College of St Hild and St Bede with Durham University released endowment money that was committed to educational purposes. It seemed to the Bishop that the two matters might be related. In May 1977 the Bishop called together a group of interested people to discuss the matter.

At first I was not invited, but when I protested to the Bishop that such plans were of primary concern to me, he invited me to share in the discussions. Three working groups were formed concerned with: clergy training, laity training and organization. The complete misunderstanding of my aims was evident in the fact that it was assumed that my interest was with laity training. No one saw that my concern was not with 'lay' people, but with the *laos* – that is with clergy and laity together and that this was fundamental to the kind of organization that was set up. I had to be pigeon-holed to fit their assumptions and their system.

Before the first meeting of the whole group I wrote a paper welcoming the possibilities of a Regional Institute and pointing out certain principles upon which I considered it should be based: people not buildings, going out rather than drawing people in, life experience as part of the data of theology, lay people helping to run the institute as well as taking part in the training, theology that starts from the issues of life.[7]

The Professor of Theology at Durham University saw rather different possibilities in the release of the Hild/Bede money. He expounded his ideas at the May meeting and afterwards developed them in a paper in which he proposed the setting up of an Institute of Christian Education with the purpose of furthering 'the education of those with responsibility for teaching the Christian faith to children. . . . The management Board of the Institute would consist of nominees of the Trustees of the College of St Hild and St Bede, representatives of the School of Education and of the Department of Theology, and representatives of participating Christian Churches in the area'.[8]

I was not the only person to be unhappy with the didactic tone of this paper and the way in which the Institute would be dominated by the University. Representatives of the Free Churches, for instance, pointed out that the kind of in-service training and lay education they needed was of a more 'home-spun' character, tailored to the fact that their financial resources were less than those of the Church of England. We were, however, arguing against a highly skilled protagonist and it was the views of Professor Sykes that prevailed.

I had been cast down by my assimilation into the structures of the Diocese of Durham. My sense of defeat and desolation was total when it became clear during these meetings that plans were taking shape around concepts far removed from my own. What seemed even worse was that no one grasped how fundamental were the differences that divided us. This seemed to be the final blow.

The North of England Institute for Christian Education, which was officially opened in 1981, in some aspects fulfils my dreams, but in others it denies them. The positive fact is that as a regional ecumenical structure it has come into being – it is there. I have to recognize that apart from the existence of NEICE the post of theological consultant would probably not have survived beyond my incumbency. The relationship of the Theological Consultancy with NEICE was a difficult issue for the group that reviewed my job. They were as worried as I was about the academic slant of the proposed institute, which seemed to contradict our aim of getting theology going at the grass roots. At the same time the Bishop of Durham made it clear that his backing for the continuation of the Theological Consultancy depended on its being related to NEICE. In their attempts to come to some agreement with those responsible for the setting up of NEICE, the Review Group got a somewhat cool reception, being viewed as a 'pressure group'. However, they persisted and as a result the Theological Consultancy, while being related to NEICE maintains a large measure of autonomy. A new consultant whose theological ability lifts the job on to a new level of possibility was appointed and started work in September 1982. All of this is positive, but it has missed an opportunity occasioned by the Archbishop's suggestion – that of co-ordinating all the theological resources of the region. Instead it has become one more organization, with its own often competing aims, alongside other bodies. While it is doing well in its own field, which is far less circumscribed than I had feared, it is not fulfilling some of the things to which I had given priority. This is particularly true with regard to having a long term policy and plan for the development and use of all the theological resources of the region. So at times I wonder 'Have we achieved the form and lost something of the substance? In striving to get a viable structure have we somehow blurred the vision? Is the institutionalized force of tradition so strong that in the end it will re-assert itself and cancel out all that is new?'

But to say that change is not possible is to deny belief in God. It is our vision of God that shapes the church. The present structure assumes that God is primarily concerned with the church. But if God's main concern is with the world and the kingdom a different structure will be needed.

The points I have made in this chapter are relevant far beyond what I have said about my own experience. There is at present much talk and planning at national level about the organization and structure of the church: the nature of the diaconate, the ordination of women, clergy training, non-stipendiary ministry and the *Tiller Report*.[9]

The overall effect of all this does *not* reflect a God whose first concern is with the world. The debate on the ordination of women focusses on matters of church order and does not consider the sense of rejection by the church and by God that many women feel. Non-stipendiary ministers are being trained for ministry in the church not in their work. Tiller proposes that more and more people should be drawn into the service of the church but does not tell us how they can be given a new vision of a God who is concerned with the world.

ACUPA is an exception to this trend in that it gives as much attention to the world as to the church. 'God' it states, 'though infinitely transcendent, is also to be found . . . in the apparent waste lands of our inner cities and housing estates.'[10] Its proposals are based on this belief and, whatever our reservations about the theological inadequacies of the report, we should welcome this change of outlook and treat the proposals positively.

If, as I am saying, the church as it is, is *not* geared to a God who is to be known and served in the world, how should it be restructured? The main points I want to stress are these:

It must be open to engage in dialogue with the world. This means listening to non-Christians as well as Christians in all aspects of life, to those who are poor and disadvantaged as well as to those who are at the creative centres of our culture.

It must affirm the ministry of lay people in their secular roles, those who are unemployed and employed, young people, retired persons. This means helping people to reflect theologically, where they are and in a systematic way. To enable this process money and persons must be made available by the church.

It means cutting out activities that are not essential to the church's main purpose; clarifying aims and stream-lining activities rather than adding a number of new side-shows.

It means that the church must be expressed in two forms, as gathered and as dispersed church. Between these two aspects of the church's life there must be dialogue, and there will inevitably be tension. But tension that is properly managed can be more creative than the 'niceness' that, because it fears conflict, excludes questions and thereby excludes discovery and growth.

None of the above proposals will be actualized unless there is planning and management. Aims must be agreed, plans must be made, resources must be reckoned, tasks must be allocated, vision must be maintained and progress must be monitored against a realistic time scale.

In matters of institutional change a very long time scale is needed, if during this time the process is to be sustained someone has to believe in a God who makes possible what seems impossible – the renewal of the church of God.

IX   What Kind of God

It is impossible to know God fully. If it were possible he would not be God. No one has been more conscious of this fact than the Jews. They refrained from uttering the name of God, for to them to know the name of a person was to assume power over that person and in some sense to control them. To claim that sort of power over God is to diminish him. The sense that God is beyond our knowing has been preserved in the Eastern Orthodox Christian tradition and is a feature of many other Eastern religions.

The Western Church has followed a more intellectualized approach. At its extreme the impression of having privileged knowledge about God is given by many earnest people who claim to 'know' God and to 'take' God into the world. A belief that they are being used by God too easily becomes a matter of using God.

A purely intellectual and conceptual approach is not enough. But that is not to say that we cannot speak about God at all. Indeed it is absolutely necessary that we do speak about God. In order to do this we must be clear about the data that is available. Two main factors are involved in a Christian understanding of God: our daily experience of life and of God, and the Christian tradition including the Bible.

Our experience comes first, our convictions about God arise out of actually meeting with God even though this may not have the kind of clarity that leads us to speak about it in those terms. What anyone can say about God, and what I am saying in this book is not opinion but testimony concerning how God has made himself known to me. This is why in this book I have tried to keep in touch with things I can speak about from first hand experience and to speak only of that 'which we have seen and heard' (I John 1.3). In this way I have found a God who shakes up any preconceived ideas about 'who he is', and indeed about who we ourselves are but who in surprising ways and often in unpromising situations shows himself to be a God of love.

Of course our experience is capable of different interpretations. We need to check our interpretations of experience against that of other people and against the testimony and understandings of Christians through the long line of tradition that goes back to the events of the life, death and resurrection of Jesus Christ as these are witnessed to in the Bible.

There is conflict about the weight that should be given to the Bible, so I must declare my own position in the matter. Our faith is not based on the Bible, but upon God who is present today as he was present in the events recorded in the Bible. The Bible is essential in that it contains witness to the events concerning Jesus and to the belief that God revealed himself in and through Jesus. The contribution of different witnesses is included and part of the authentication of the truth of their witness lies paradoxically in the fact that they do not agree about just what happened or how these events should be understood. It is left to us to respond to their witness out of our own experience of God and in the light of our own interpretations. This means that, just as we need to check our understandings of life against the Bible, so we also need to check the understandings of God that come to us from the Bible against our present experience of God. Though the Bible is essential we cannot turn to it for a simple answer to the question: 'What kind of God?'

Talk about God comes out of experience of God. Such talk cannot be a factual description of God but must be in an indirect form of metaphors, pictures and models. To speak of God in the images for instance of 'shepherd' or 'fire' is to recapture an experience of God not to suggest that God *is* a shepherd or *is* fire.

The kind of models we use are those that resonate with experience and that point towards that which is beyond experience – God. The only models we can use are those that are available to us in our culture.

I have constantly referred to the fact that there are in operation, conflicting models of Christian faith. In looking at the question 'What kind of God?' in this chapter, I begin by discussing models of God. My conviction is that our present problem about God lies not in the conflict of competing models, but in the fact that our conception of God is dominated by so few models. To make matters worse, those that are in use do not resonate with people's experience of God or insights into life. This leads to a divorce between God and life and a distorted and restricted view of God.

Certain models are being used as if they were actual descriptions of God. The God the image is meant to illuminate is identified with the image, so that an idolatrous image takes the place of the living God. In order to expand our understanding and experience of God the 'idols' that we have erected must be broken and other models must be brought into use.

Not only have we got too few models but we have the wrong models. The models that people naturally use are those that make sense in their particular society. Such models effect a two-way process of validation between characteristics of the social set-up and aspects of God's nature. In an agrarian society, for instance, it makes sense to talk of God as 'husbandman' and 'vinedresser', and these images give religious significance to a rural way of life. In a more developed society God is more easily pictured as Lord and King.

In our urban/industrial society a few models: Lord, Master, King, Father, dominate our conception of God. These models have seemed to make sense of and to validate our particular kind of society. Complex as the relationship is, it is clear that religion is a factor in creating and supporting the values of an industrial society: heirarchical organization, obedience to external authority, paternalism, dependence on the 'benign' domination of the *male* 'Father' figure.

Now it is becoming obvious that the exclusive use of these models is distorting our understanding of God and inhibiting the contribution Christianity might make to human and social development. The qualities these models stress contradict the most creative insights of today: participation, the responsibility and power of human beings, human solidarity, the equality of women and men.

In order to open up our understanding of God we must forge new models. Mindful of the fact that most religious experience today is not specifically Christian, we should explore the wealth of imagery that is available in human experience and in the world's religions, and we must rediscover the images embedded in the Hebraic/Christian tradition. There is so much in our tradition that we overlook.

One model that could get us on to a new line of thought is that which runs right through Hebrew thinking about God – 'wind'.

God cannot be seen, but his presence and activity in the world has real effects. These can be terrifying as in a storm, or refreshing as with a breeze. God as 'breath' (the same Hebrew word 'ruach'), was seen as the source of life: (God) 'breathed into his nostrils the breath of life, and man became a living being' (Gen. 2.7).

The wind/breath/spirit image is helpful in that it conveys something of how people actually experience God: invisible, but effective in his activity in people and in the world, all pervasive, free, unpredictable, not to be seen as one object among other objects, not to be controlled by man and not to be compared with man. The image resonates with ordinary human experience and 'wind' and 'breath' are basic human images.

In Hebrew thinking the Spirit is God himself, present and active in the world, inspiring in people all sorts of creativity and empowering the prophets. Israel looked forward to an ideal time when God's spirit would be poured out on all people: 'Then justice will dwell in the wilderness and righteousness abide in the fruitful field' (Isa. 32.16 and the whole chapter).

It was in line with this tradition that the Spirit of God was believed to be active in the life of Jesus Christ, and that through him the Spirit came in power to the disciples after the resurrection. The force of this model is its emphasis on the freedom of God and his power to free people.

Other models such as 'fire', 'depth', 'the all' have been explored recently by theologians in an attempt to get away from the limitations of an idea of God imposed by an exclusive use of anthropomorphic images. There impersonal models loosen things up. They do not emphasize the control of a dominant Father figure with the consequent pressure for a tightly ordered society, but allow room for variety, creativity and change. They free people from the sense that there are set rules to which they must conform and let them explore their own potentialities. At the same time the use of impersonal models has led to accusations on two counts: running into the danger of pantheism, and doing away with the sense of a personal God. Pantheism suggests that God not only pervades everything, but that he is no more than everything. In this way it leaves no place for the transcendence of God. This important point must be borne in mind in the course of this discussion. The question of God as personal will be pursued now.

All of us feel a deep need to be loved and valued for ourselves as we are as unique persons irreplaceable by any other person. In addition to (not instead of) the impersonal we need personal models of God. In Christian faith this need is met in the person of Jesus Christ.

Jesus Christ is for all Christians central to their faith, but he is understood in many different ways. For instance today one outcome of the odd relationship between religion and society is that most people see religion as a purely personal matter and many see it in terms of a personal relationship with Jesus. Something has gone wrong when, rather than being seen as 'the way' to a God who pervades the whole world, Jesus is seen as God, and as *all there is to God*. This 'Jesus' may be the answer to my need, but he is not the answer to the *world's* need.

We must go beyond this cosy 'Jesuology' and see Jesus not only in his relationship with individuals, but in his relationship with the world, with humanity and with God.

In the incarnation God entered into the world and into human life, but many people still insist on removing God from the world.

The majority of Christians only accept the humanity of Jesus with qualifications: 'If Jesus was God he knew everything', 'Jesus died on the cross as part of God's plan'. 'He knew (as we do) that it would all come right in the end'. By this kind of argument Jesus' life is removed from the processes of this world. His death and resurrection become symbols to be understood only in figurative terms, and God does not meet our need except in general and abstract terms. Human response has nothing to do with action that might change anything in this world, but only with interior changes in the individual. All we need is 'faith', and if things go wrong for our world it is attributed to lack of faith: 'If nations accepted Christianity they would not be in their present mess!' If young people were brought up in Christian homes there would be no juvenile delinquency!'

Jesus has ceased to be human and become an example of abstract 'perfection'. He is projected as always being in control of his situation, and any suggestion of weakness is explained away. Yet Jesus, weeping over Jerusalem, washing his disciples feet, asking them to pray with him, suggests a God who does not dominate, but serves and shares and calls others to do the same. In this the gospels support a different ethos for society, and show Jesus living by relationships that are different from those that are structured into our society. It is for instance false to what the Gospels say about Mary's activities to hold up Jesus' relationship with his mother as that of a dutiful son to a stay-at-home mother! We need to look at the Gospels again and find other models that are in them. One model that I find helpful in calling out a sense of risk and adventure is that of 'Jesus the *pioneer* of our faith' (Heb. 12.2; 2.10). The epistle to the Hebrews in which this model occurs makes it clear that for Jesus pioneering was a real struggle that involved 'prayers, supplications, with loud cries and tears' (Heb. 5.7).

A dismissive attitude to the humanity of Jesus and to his involvement in the mechanisms of history, denies significance to all humanity and all history. Of course there are problems about the historical details of Jesus' life. Historical criticism has put a question mark against what we may or may not know. We may find this confusing but it does not help us to approach the Gospels as if each statement is a literal statement of fact. Nor would it help even if we had every detail about Jesus' words and actions. What the Gospel writers give us is testimony concerning what Jesus meant to them. The fact that the form in which we receive it reflects the situation of the churches for whom each Gospel was written is in itself historical data, for it tells us what Jesus continued to mean for a new generation.

We cannot of course make what we like of Jesus. It is the Jesus who lived and died, who in his risen life is present to us. It was important that after his resurrection Jesus identified himself to the disciples as the same Jesus who had been cricified, 'See my hands and my feet, that it is I myself, handle me and see' (Luke 24.39). The memory of Jesus of Nazareth enables us to identify the living Christ present with us now. Historical criticism clarifies what is significant and in spite of the questions it raises, its overall result is 'to establish the basic traits of Jesus with at least moral certainty'.[1]

A further obstacle to understanding the meaning of Jesus Christ, is that, though the world is being forced to recognize the interdependence of all people, Christians remain obstinately individualistic. They are unable to see that by entering the world in one human life, God entered into the life of all humanity. God in Jesus Christ did not become a man, but man. The point that has to be grasped is that in and through Jesus Christ God has become present in the whole world and in all humanity. If God is to be found anywhere he must be found in and through 'ordinary' things and 'ordinary' people. Our search for God must be, not primarily by considering 'religious' matters, but by digging deeply into human experience (see Chapter III). Jesus is not all there is to God. We have to see Jesus in his relationship of oneness with the Father. People glibly say 'Jesus is God', as though they already knew what they mean by God. But it is the other way round, we do not interpret the life of Jesus in the light of some prior knowledge of God, but we come to know God through Jesus Christ. Jesus contradicted and continues to contradict people's ideas about God. God is not who *we* want him to be, or who *we* think he ought to be. God is as he is in Jesus Christ.

To be a human being is to find oneself immersed in and having to respond to a given situation. In Jesus' situation people had certain insights and expectations concerning God and the eschatological kingdom of God. There was a belief that God would intervene to set right the injustices of the world. Hope was seen for the future as present sufferings were identified with the woes that would herald the ending of the present era and the dawning of God's eternal reign of peace, harmony, *Shalom*. With these high hopes were mixed beliefs that they themselves would be proved right, and their enemies destroyed.

There was (as in all situations) sin, not just in individuals but with external embodiments that gave shape and structure to the overall situation. Pride, self-aggrandisement, subservience to the occupying power, hardness towards the common people were embodied not only in secular but in the religious institutions and in those who officially represented God.

In these particular circumstances, through his outlook, actions, preaching and denunciations, Jesus raised the question of the authentic reality of God. Was God actually on the side of the Jewish people regardless of their behaviour? Was God really like his official representatives and what they taught about him, or had they got it wrong?

By posing the question of God Jesus was set on a collision course with the religious authorities. By pursuing the question Jesus' life became a journey to the cross. His crucifixion came out of the specific circumstances of his life and out of his journey towards the discovery and revelation of God.

The relationship between Jesus and the Father is for Christians most difficult to comprehend when it comes to the cross: Was Jesus abandoned by the Father? Some concepts of God emphasize the impassiveness of God, and some theories of the atonement picture the Father as offering the Son as a 'price' for the redemption of the world. In our money-orientated society the image conjured up is that of the pawn-shop. To the first Christians the experience of liberation came first, and in struggling to express this experience the image they used was that of slaves chained for sale in the market being released to become free human beings. Their emphasis was on the experience of being free and they knew that this is effected by a love that comes from God. To suggest that the Father acted apart from the Son is to suggest a God who is monstrously unfeeling and immoral. Such a view drives a wedge between a heartless Father and a suffering Son.

Was Jesus as God, so sure of God, that he was able to bear his sufferings in the knowledge that it would all come right in the end? If that was the case Jesus would not have shared fully in human life, and a wedge would be driven between God and humanity.

But God does care about us and Father and Son are at one. Jesus suffered the real experience of being abandoned by God. 'My God, My God why hast thou forsaken me?' is the cry of humanity against a God who seems absent and ineffective when we need him most. But the Father suffers too as he suffers with the Son and in the suffering of the Son. God participates in and is affected by the sufferings of history and through the Son takes into himself all the pain and suffering of the world.

From a position of comfort Christians speak easily about God as love. This cuts little ice with the man who after serving a firm faithfully for years suddenly finds himself on the scrapheap, or the youngsters whose lives fall apart as parents, who had promised to 'love until death us do part', take other partners, the millions who starve in a world of plenty or the many who are imprisoned just because they struggle for justice. Only a God who suffers with humanity can meet the needs of humanity.

To say that God is in the world could lead to a falsely optimistic view of the world. The cross brings us up against the reality of human suffering and faces us with God's judgment on the sin that causes it. Jesus on the cross reveals the credibility of God as love. On the cross God is seen to be totally committed to people.

A crucified God contradicts all previous ideas about God and in particular it puts in question assumptions about God's power. The images Lord, Master, King suggest a particular kind of power that is summed up in the popular view of God as 'almighty', fully in control, loving, creating and redeeming without effort, from outside the world. Of course Christians have always been told that God limits the exercise of his power in order to preserve the possibility of a free human response to his love. 'But the impression has still been given that, if he wanted to, he could summon his legions of angels, could smite the earth, (or York Minster)[2] with his thunderbolts, and indeed quite often does intervene directly in the affairs of men and in the course of nature.'[3]

But God's power is not like that, and Jesus' contradiction of this view put him at variance with his contemporaries. The question is not so much about the reality of God's power, but for what purposes and how he uses it. Different kinds of power serve different purposes.

Jesus' temptations may be seen as a struggle within himself about how to use power for God's purposes. His opponents feared his power and his closest friends were disappointed at the fact that he did not use his power as they thought it should be used. His response was negative when they wanted him to turn the tables on their national enemies, 'Wilt thou at this time restore the Kingdom to Israel?' (Acts 1.6); and he combatted the idea that discipleship was a way to status and power. In response to the request from James and John 'Grant us to sit one at your right hand and one at your left, in your glory' (Mark 10.37), Jesus gave a new definition of greatness:

> Those who are supposed to rule over the Gentiles lord it over them, and their great men exercise authority over them. But it shall not be so among you: but whoever would be great among you must be your servant (Mark 10.42–43).

The question was whether power was to be used to crush enemies and thus lead to new forms of oppression; to exalt one group of people over another and thus create new divisions between people; or to free people from the real oppressions under which they suffer, including their own attitudes of revenge and self-doubt *for* community and communion.

External power may achieve the first two aims, but for the last purpose a more fundamental change is needed – a change of heart. Neither Jesus' friends nor his enemies understood this, and right up to the time of his death they expected that God would at last show his power by some miraculous intervention. But this did not happen and Jesus' death on the cross reveals love as the only power God has.

But can love actually change anything? Or are we, by saying that love is the only power God has, suggesting that God is powerless? Today many people have cause to feel hopeless about the future. To take a local example – for people in the mining communities of County Durham there is little to hope for after the closure of their pits. Within these communities there is bitterness as a result of the long strike and division between 'scabs' and 'strikers'. Their future is in the hands of institutions – government, Coal Board, Unions, which seem incapable of new thinking or action. Creativity is quenched by individual power struggles and constant disappointments. The world scene is equally hopeless as relationships between nations sink into a vicious circle of tit-for-tat.

Resurrection is the promise that things can be different. By raising Jesus from the dead God shows his love as *saving* power. Love is saving power or saving grace in that it does what no other form of power can do, it breaks the vicious circles of sin and creates new life. In order to understand how this can be 'good news' for our world we must get rid of two common confusions concerning the resurrection of Jesus and what it promises for us:

First, resurrection is *not* the 'happy ending' that allows us to forget the misery of the world. Instead it draws us more deeply into that misery, for crucifixion and resurrection are linked and it is *out* of the misery that God brings new life. God is *in* the pain and sin of the world, but he is not trapped, as we are, in it, for God is not only in the world, he also transcends the world and is therefore able to free us from the past for newness of life.

Secondly, resurrection is not just about life after death for the individual. It is about the transformation of the whole world. To see things from this perspective we must understand the viewpoint from which the New Testament accounts of Jesus' resurrection were written. Jesus' resurrection was understood on the basis of the eschatology of the time. This is not to say that ideas were taken over wholesale. What they did was to provide a framework which, in the light of the reality of Jesus, underwent radical change. In this framework there was no expectation of the resurrection of one individual. Where the resurrection idea occurred it was as a universal hope for the restoration of all things. The image that stood for this renewal was the kingdom of God. In the risen Jesus his followers believed that the kingdom of God had come, for had not the eyes of the blind been opened, and the ears of the deaf unstopped, and the poor had the good news preached to them? (Isa. 35.5/Luke 7.22). Did not Jesus himself represent the new humanity in which God's own spirit dwelt?

But things did not turn out according to past expectations. The world did not come to a speedy end with the inauguration of the kingdom; and Christians were left with a new question: What is the relation between these eschatological events and our earthly history? From that time they lived in a tension between two realities – the kingdom present now and promised for the future and a world in which evil, suffering and death still had power. To this question they found a new answer: Jesus is the pioneer of a new humanity. His resurrection is a beginning not an end of the new creation. It is a sign that God will fulfil his purpose, a promise and possibility for the world and for history. His resurrection founds a history that can and ought to be lived out.

To make real what is promised in the resurrection of Jesus means living in the power of God's Spirit. A new outpouring of the Spirit of God on all flesh was part of the eschatological expectation. This, it was believed, happened through Jesus Christ. In the Fourth Gospel Jesus' resurrection is affirmed as the beginning of new creation, in the explicit link that is made between the receiving of the Spirit by Jesus' followers and the Genesis story of creation:

> [Jesus] breathed on them and said to them, 'Receive the Holy Spirit' (John 20.22 cf. Gen. 1 and 2).

In Acts the images of 'wind' and 'fire' that are used of God's Spirit in the Old Testament are picked up:

> And suddenly a sound came from heaven like the rush of a mighty wind . . . and there appeared unto them tongues as of fire, distributed and resting on each one of them. And they were all filled with the Holy Spirit (Acts 2.2–4).

The power of God in the world is the power of God's love in us and among us:

> . . . God's love has been poured into our hearts through the Holy Spirit which has been given to us (Rom. 5.5).

God, who through his Spirit brought the world into being, is also active in new creation.

In the New Testament there is a flexibility in describing the Spirit – the Spirit of God, the Spirit of His Son, the Spirit of Jesus, Holy Spirit, Spirit of Truth. This points to the fact that, although there are different experiences of God, there are no hard divisions between Father, Son and Spirit. There is only one God, but he is not a one-dimensional God. God is more than we can conceive through any one experience or any one image. And this brings me back to the matter of images and to the question of whether we should think of God as personal or impersonal. I suggested that 'wind' and 'breath' are useful images in that they do not share the limitations of human images. The conclusion should not be drawn from this that, while God (Father, Son) may be spoken of in personal terms as 'He' or 'She', the Spirit is an impersonal 'It'. It is not a matter of using either personal or impersonal images, but of using both (She, He, It). By super-imposing images on each other we may see God as personal and as more than *a* person. In our experience of God, the Father continues as the transcendent nameless God, the Son is the historical appearance of the Father who makes clear in history how one responds to the Father, and the Spirit is God in us and among us. The Spirit is the continual pouring out of God's creating and re-creating love on the world, and the work of the Spirit is the incorporation of the individual and of all people into the life and work of God.

It is within this understanding of God in his relationships with the world and in his promises for the world that the church must understand herself.

All the accounts of Jesus' appearances stress a mission for his followers. He calls them to share in a mission that is not the church's mission but the mission of God through his Spirit. God's Spirit inspires people to share in the movement that makes God's resurrection promises real in history.

Christians easily take a proprietary view of the Spirit as though it belonged only to them. When they are told that God's Spirit is poured out not just on a chosen few but on *all* flesh, they experience an identity problem. If people, who do not acknowledge God or Jesus Christ, are working for the kingdom's ideals of justice, peace and human solidarity, what is the place of the church? God as Spirit is everywhere present creating and sustaining all things and all people. His love is constantly seeking a response, but each one is free to respond or to be deaf to his call, and not all people respond. Many who do respond serve God's kingdom without knowing *who* it is they serve. The church consists of those who acknowledge that God is who he has shown himself to be in Jesus Christ.

The distinctive and vital feature of the church is therefore that, though many may serve God's purposes in history, the church alone knows the meaning of what is happening in history.

The church's task is to explain the world to itself. This it must do in the light of its eschatology – that is to say its understanding of what God has revealed of his eternal purposes for the world and for humanity. There is no need to despair of the world for God's promise of the kingdom is that the whole world shall move towards justice, peace and community. In this purpose God wills to work through people and empowers them through his Spirit, so that already there are many signs in the world of the kingdom.

In the traumas of change we should not be overcome with fear, but should recognize that choices are being opened up by which, if rightly made, things can move forward to the kingdom. In our particular circumstances we are called to make judgments for the kingdom and against injustice, factions, war, oppression, enmity, division. If we make our choice against the kingdom or fail to make any judgment at all, God himself will be our judge. In his judgment God will make it plain that certain things simply will not do. If, for instance, we continue to dump every kind of rubbish in the sea, we shall have a major environmental and health problem on our hands. If we do not give equal opportunities to people in the inner cities, including the ethnic minorities, we shall all suffer from riots and rebellion. In Jesus' parables of the kingdom the point is made that a decision for or against the kingdom is a decision for or against Jesus himself. The stories are of everyday matters of people at work in the fields and at home, or going on a journey, and in each story it is made clear that one cannot sit on the fence – in one's attitude or action one declares oneself to be for or against the kingdom, for or against Jesus – Jesus and the kingdom should not be separated for Jesus is the Christ, that is the eschatological man, the one anointed with God's Spirit, pioneer of the new humanity through whom the kingdom comes into being.

The church's gospel is that Jesus is the Christ, and that through him the transformation of the world is being effected. It is therefore through the proclamation of Jesus as Christ that the church brings hope to a world that, through the failure of misplaced hopes, is without hope.

Many people ask the question 'Where is the world going?': and the answer assumed is 'To destruction! and there is nothing *we* can do about it'.

Christians give a different answer. While recognizing that the situation is critical, as indeed it always has been and will be, they see hope for the future. Believing in Jesus as the Christ who reveals God's purposes for the world, they take heart and work with others and with God for the transformation of the world. Their answer to the question 'Where is the world going?' is – 'to God and the kingdom'.

This book is about God and the answer to the question 'What kind of God?' In the course of it I have said a good deal about the church. The reason for this is that the church is a visible sign of God's presence in the world, and in itself it should express the character of God and his kingdom. What Christians are and what the church is expresses more· powerfully than any words *who* their God is. All people have in themselves a need and a capacity for God, and there are in the world *and* in the church many gods and substitutes for God. The church must be clear what kind of God it proclaims and it should be like its God. If God loves the world, if Jesus gave himself for the world, if the Spirit permeates the world, then the church must do likewise. In its love for the world it must give itself for the world and permeate the world by sharing with others in the transformation of the world. It is as it does this that through its outlook, actions, preachings and denunciations, it must, like Jesus, raise the question of God. Following the way of Jesus the church by what it is, what it does and what it says, must give credibility to God as love. This it can only do if all the time it is alert to God who continually questions its own understandings of him by showing in the life of the world what love demands and what love is.

X   Journeying On

At the beginning of this book I said that my aim was to help people to discover God in life. As a theological consultant my work involves helping people to reflect on their own experience of God in the light of Christian tradition, so that they may come to a clearer understanding of the truth about God and so walk confidently and faithfully in the way of discipleship. At the same time I have emphasized that God is not to be known by purely intellectual means and that he remains a hidden God. Just as we cannot get to know a person by abstract study and can never know them in any conclusive sense, so – and even more so, we can never unlock the mystery of God, only at the end by God's grace and mercy shall we see him as he is. Meanwhile God addresses his revelation to faith, and faith can never be imposed upon the mind by rational argument.

The revelation that is given, however, is enough for God's immediate purpose. Through it he calls people to embark on a journey of faith, to step out from the security of what they know into the unknown. By taking such a step they enter upon new experiences of God.

But there is a place for rational reflection and argument, that is for the specifically theological task:

> In the light of his experience of faith, the believer will meditate upon God's word, His loving union with God will refine his discernment. He may order his knowledge of revelation, reflect upon it, draw out its implications and attempt, when useful, a reformation of various statements. Such activity is fruitful, it allows what he believes to penetrate into his mind and enter into relation with the rest of his experience.[1]

To help people see how faith in God has implications for all their experience and in doing this to re-form their images of God was at the heart of my task as theological consultant.

The interpretation of revealed truth, for the reasons stated above, presents an insoluble problem for unaided human intelligence. Flashes of insight may be given to all sorts of people, but these remain incoherent, possibly leading to fixed positions and extreme polarizations, unless they are seen within a tradition and checked by a community.

This brings me back to the issue of 'church'. Ideally the church should be the community within which, in a spirit of waiting on God, what is revealed about God is interpreted.

God reveals himself in many ways, in the hearts of individuals, in our experiences of him, and in the events of history, but the meaning of what he reveals is ambiguous. The church's task is to interpret this meaning, for in Jesus Christ it has the clue to human life and to history. This is not to say that the church has a clear theory of where history is going, for Jesus Christ is not a system but a person. Jesus' grasp of the truth about history came from his knowledge of God, a truth that was mediated to him through his Jewish religious tradition, through his own reflections on the tradition and through his experience of living in a trusting relationship with God.

There is no knock down argument about the end and purposes of history, only a belief that is based on belief in God.

Christians cannot find a clue to history in the person of Jesus if they do not accept his full humanity. Too often they shunt him 'off in a Godward direction (God himself having already been edged out of the world of man) so that Jesus too ceases to have any critical impact on the life of the world'.[2] But Jesus proclaimed God's cause to be the cause of humanity, and the end of history to be the completion of the one true humanity, of which Jesus himself is the pioneer.

What the final kingdom will be like we cannot imagine. We do, however, get glimpses of it in Jesus' parables and in his practice of the kingdom as he forgives sinners, heals the sick, feeds the hungry, welcomes the outcasts and attacks all that destroys humanity. Though we are unable to imagine positively what the final kingdom will be like, we do know from our negative experiences what it will *not* be like. In the kingdom of God there will *not*, for instance, be war with all its horrors, children dying of leukemia, leaking roofs or broken homes. God's will is to do away with such evils. With God and believing in God we shall attack the specific forms of inhumanity which appear in our world. In doing this we become participants in creating a positive and meaningful history. Interpretation and response, theology and praxis belong together. There can be no credibility in a gospel for humanity that does not strive in practical ways against all that denies humanity. There are different views about what it means to be human, what kind of future is possible, and *how* things can be changed. Christians have a specific perspective on these matters which comes from belief in God as he is revealed in Jesus Christ. From this perspective the church should help people to understand and respond to their experience in the world.

But the church is *not* doing this. Many of the people I worked with, far from being helped to understand their lives in terms of the reality of God, had been made to feel that God was not interested in their lives. In their contacts with the church they had not been opened up to fuller life, but had had a spiritual and intellectual strait-jacket imposed on them.

A second and related task for the church is to help people grow spiritually, yet prayer for many Christians is still at the level only of 'asking'. The essence of Christian prayer is a deepening communion with God, and for this we need not only to know God but to know ourselves.

Many 'secular' insights and skills are available today which help people become more aware of their inner feelings and motives and discover themselves as individuals in relation to others. These should be used by the church in addition to its own traditional resources, in opening people to the meaning and practice of prayer.

Jesus' inner life was nurtured by the spiritual tradition of the Jews, which saw the focus of prayer as a whole-hearted search for the will of God. In line with the prophets Jesus perceived that God's will is different from what is generally accepted to be 'right' even by religious leaders. His prayer involved a struggle to align his own will with the will of God and to maintain his oneness with God.

In some crucial respects Jesus departed from his tradition, notably in the fact that he spoke to God quite simply and directly as 'Abba', 'Dad'. Talking with God was in Jesus' practice natural and not hedged about with protocol. If we can enter into this relationship of absolute trust in God we shall not feel the need to justify ourselves by our works, or experience identity problems, for we shall know that God accepts us *as we are*.

People are not all alike and the Christian spiritual tradition contains rich and varied experiences of all sorts of people in all sorts of circumstances, it has something for each of us.

Though each person must make their own spiritual journey, the full experience of 'God with us' is communal. (It is communal rather than collective because each person brings their own gifts into the group. If on the other hand people have not been helped to discover themselves, worship becomes a matter of external conformity and collectivity.) It is where two or three are gathered together in his name that Jesus is present in the midst. That is to say that it is primarily in our experience as 'church' that we are invited to enter into communion with each other and with God. The church is the eschatological community which already celebrates 'God with us' and, as proper complement to its struggles in and for the world, the church waits for the kingdom.

But this tradition of contemplation and struggle is not being opened up as a resource. Though Christians are exhorted to pray, little help is given to them as to how they should pray, nor are conditions provided in which they may learn to pray. A prayer at the beginning of a meeting may help people to recollect themselves and to be open to God's Spirit during the meeting, but on the other hand it may be no more than a formality.

Formal prayer in many of the groups I worked with would have been counter-productive, but in these groups there was mutual support in a common search for truth and for God. I am not suggesting that this is enough, but it underlines the fact that much of the mutual support for personal, practical, intellectual and spiritual journeying comes from *outside* local church congregations.

Each of us needs to belong to some grouping within which we can know people personally and in which attention can be given to us as persons. This need is not automatically covered by membership of a local congregation. I believe we should encourage all sorts of groupings of faith, action, reflection, prayer and endurance. Some of these may and should be coterminous with a local congregation, but many will have no such affiliation. Some will be long term but others will be more in the nature of support parties brought into being for a particularly hazardous stretch of the journey and then dispersed.

Such groups are intermediate groups in that, though they do not offer all that is implied by 'church', they do in some way relate Christian tradition to the life and concerns of their members. There is a proper concern for the unity of the church, which many people fear is threatened by the multiplication of groups. We should not of course equate any particular group with 'church', but structure and conformity will not in itself guarantee unity.

The one thing that unifies all Christians is Jesus Christ and discipleship of Jesus Christ. This is why it is important that in these provisional groups there is an honest attempt to come to terms with the Christian tradition as it bears upon life. If this is to be done helpfully there is need for an even deeper understanding of the tradition than may be needed in more settled conditions, for there must be a flexibility in handling Christian belief so that appropriate nourishment is made available for people with different needs and at different stages of their journey. The groups should not harden into ends in themselves which fix people at a certain stage of their development, but should expect people to move in or out as their needs change. The existence of such groups should be seen as an enrichment of the concept of 'church' by representing what I have pointed to as necessary expressions of the church in the world. They should be a means by which the church, instead of freezing people into conformity, enables growth, variety and movement. A church that is supportive of movement in the ways I have suggested points to a God who is himself on the move, calling us forward and with us in journeying.

The important thing is that we should not settle down where we are but should keep moving, with others and with God – towards God.

I began this book by describing part of my own spiritual journey. I will end by making some brief comments on my progress since then.

I described in Chapter I what was a fairly overwhelming experience of God, to which I found it difficult to respond until I was brought into touch with the Christian tradition and with a local Christian community. In spite of all my negative comments about the church as it is, I acknowledge my continuing debt to the institutional church. Its ordered life and worship form a framework within which our inarticulate responses find expression and feelings are channelled. The individual is linked into an immediate physical fellowship which is part of a world-wide fellowship of the Spirit, which includes many who have no 'membership ticket'.

I continue to worship in my local church and to minister as an accredited lay worker of the church.

Without the church the memory of Jesus Christ would be lost. Christian tradition, however, is not unchanging but develops as the followers of Jesus, in the Spirit of Jesus, respond to new situations. In recent years I have gained new insights into the mystery of life and of God by: working for a short time in Nigeria and sharing life with those who have few of the comforts of the West; meeting with people of other faiths in our own cities; taking part in a community development project in which the gifts of working class women were being discovered and used; and learning from feminists how much my own attitudes have been shaped by the masculine mores of the church. These experiences have made me look critically at what I have received by way of Christian tradition. What, for instance, am I to make of the fact that as I meet and pray with people of other faiths I recognize in them the Spirit of the same God who makes himself known in Jesus Christ? The growth in understanding that has been stimulated by these experiences has been further helped by reading what others have made of similar challenges to their faith, especially books that give new perspectives on the revelation of God in Jesus Christ. (I have already mentioned some of these books such as *Christology at the Crossroads* by Jon Sobrino and *Jesus* by Schillebeeckx). Reading is one way of sharing in the world-wide fellowship of 'church'.

New understandings must be linked to practical response to God's promise of the kingdom, and God continues to reveal himself and his purposes to us in new ways as we respond to the events of our world. Recently for instance, I spent a day with a group of people from Consett, a town which since the closure of its steelworks in 1980 has faced massive unemployment. The people I was with were managers and supervisers of Community Programmes (funded by the Manpower Services Commission.) The programmes provide work useful to the community for unemployed people for one year. In our discussion a good deal of frustration was expressed at the seemingly arbitrary way in which Government and MSC organize and disorganize the scheme. But through all the frustrations and the apparent hopelessness of the situation, my over-riding feeling was of a group of people who were discovering in themselves new resources of imagination, concern for others and endurance as they created in Consett a new kind of community. In all the darkness I saw signs of the kingdom of God. They were not all church people but they invited me, as a theologian to help them understand their situation, so that by what they did they could literally make sense of it. Together we took a step in that direction. On the same lines and more continuously I share in the 'Respond' project. This deals with similar issues in Cleveland as people try to make sense of the different aspects of a changing society; unemployment, poverty, the use of leisure, changing sex roles and so on.

In my early experience I related how I discovered God as one who could meet *my* need. Now, though I am just as aware of my dependence on God, I try to share his concern for the world in all its conflicts, need, stupidity and suffering. I endeavour to 'stand by God in *his* hour of grieving'.[3]

New experiences have potential for spiritual growth. If prayer is to be more than a matter of duty the imagination needs to be awakened. In this respect I have been helped by sharing in a retreat for handicapped people, in which I discovered their special gifts of awareness of God and my own hardness of heart towards 'the least'. I did not find the communal experience of prayer that I looked for in any local prayer group, but in group meditations that took place at a Roman Catholic House of Prayer and more fleetingly at a parish retreat on Holy Island.

As far as mutual support goes I no longer have a formal advisory group, though I am still in touch with its two remaining members. My work in this region and beyond has linked me into a network of people with whom over the years and in a variety of co-operations I have shared a common search for God and for faithfulness to his purposes. I continue to be in touch with many of these people in what I hope is a mutually supportive relationship. In addition and importantly I am a member of a geographically widespread but close knit family.

Finally, the emotional upheaval which was part of my early experience is not a necessary part of everyone's journey. As a long distance walker, I know that it is not possible to bounce along all the way. What matters is that, using whatever direction finding equipment is available, and rejoicing in companionship on the way, we journey on. . . .

Appendices

Appendix I

On the Appointment of a Theological Consultant in Industrial and Social Affairs

The Post: Theological consultant in industrial and social affairs to the Bishop of Durham and in the North East.

Background to the post: It is the task of the Christian church to make available to the men of each age and every culture the fulness of God's self-giving embodied in Jesus Christ.

Such a task presupposes utter fidelity to all that is given in Christ and a sensitive awareness of the human condition in each age and place.

The theologian is at the service of the church in this task – his scrutiny and systematic reflection extending on the one hand to the data of revelation (signifying God's intentions for man) and on the other hand to the gamut of human problems (showing man's need of God), and including a consideration of how these two are to be related to one another.

In an area such as the North East of England, men's problems take their specific characteristic form in the context of a particular type of developing industrial society. This has given rise to certain difficulties for every type of mission or pastoral enterprise undertaken by the church, whether of the more traditional, parochial kind, or of more recent design (of which Industrial Mission is only one, though perhaps the most significant).

It is clear that if the church is to perform effectively its task of communicating Christian faith as a way of life to the people of this region today, it needs the assistance of a theology geared to the real situation – (a theology lest it fall into sheer pragmatism, and geared to the reality, lest it fail by irrelevance).

The appointment of a theological consultant in industrial and social affairs to the Bishop of Durham and in the North East is one contribution towards meeting this need.

The appointee is responsible to the Bishop of Durham.

However, since it is recognized that any strategy of the church must take into account the urban development on both sides of the Tyne and Tees, the Bishop of Durham has negotiated, on behalf of the appointee, certain relationships with the Archbishop of York and with the Bishop of Newcastle. It is also clear that any forward theological thinking must engage people of all denominations, and it is hoped that the appointee will operate with official ecumenical backing.

Specific tasks: These can be divided into two kinds, theological research projects and certain forms of collaboration.

(a) *Research Projects*

1. To examine the whole body of Christian teaching with particular concern for the problem of how it is to be communicated to the people of the North-East Region.

2. To examine in particular the theological foundations of the work of the church in industrial society with special reference to the North East.

3. To make a systematic survey of the questions that industry and technological change are raising in society throughout the area covered by the Diocese of Durham, Teesside and Tyneside.

4. To collect, correlate, develop and clarify the theological insights gained by any of the church's mission enterprises in the area (including the Industrial Missions), with a view to (i) making these available to those involved in the formation of clergy and Christian laymen, and (ii) indicating how these insights can help to increase the effectiveness of the enterprises.

(b) *Collaborations*

1. To relate in particular to the work of the Industrial Missions in the area, taking into account their ecumenical nature, with a view to (i) helping them to deepen the theological foundation upon which the work can continue to develop, and (ii) sharing in the planning and execution of agreed schemes for the training of personnel (clerical and lay) working with the missions.

2. To ensure, with reference to the appropriate boards and committees, that theological discussion of the social and industrial affairs of the area is ecumenical in character, and that it benefits from the contributions of universities, theological colleges and technical colleges.

3. To help promote, under the auspices of the appropriate boards and committees discussion between people of various disciplines and groups formative of society and theological scholarship throughout the area with a view to (i) sharing and developing research material with others and (ii) forming a cadre of people (clerical and lay) who will help others reflect theologically in the context of North-East society.

4. To relate to other special ministries to society as may be mutually agreed for similar purposes as in (b 1).

Appendix II

Secular Experience and Theological Thinking[1]

One important purpose of theology is that it should help people in particular situations to understand the situation better and respond more appropriately.

This is an aspect of theology with which I am particularly concerned for I am continually seeing people struggling and not being helped. Some examples will show the sort of thing I mean.

A local councillor told me how his party, which was the controlling party in the council, decided to re-house the people of an area where there was a high level of atmospheric pollution. The opposing party used the occasion to capture votes for themselves, stirring up trouble in the area, and leading to a situation of conflict on the council, in which there was a great deal of bitterness and emotional irrationality. The councillor wanted to know what bearing his Christian faith has on the situation and how he can continue to do what he believes to be right for the people of the area, without being obsessed with the negative elements of the conflict, and how he can bring a more constructive attitude into the proceedings of the council as a whole.

In this case a few of us were able to work with him towards an answer to his questions. The way in which we did this and our conclusions are of course important, but at this point I simply want to underline the fact that I believe there is a crucial role for theology in this kind of situation. Many laymen are in similar positions of responsibility and tension, but they are not helped to see how Christian faith can be relevant, or how they can make a specifically Christian contribution within secular groups.

Even in the realm of personal problems, where it is often assumed that Christianity has most to say, things are no better. I was told of a woman who went to a psychiatrist, because of problems in her relationship with her mother-in-law. The psychiatrist saw that her problem was connected with the fact that she had been brought up to believe in love as an absolute commandment without however being helped to understand what 'love' is. When constant friction developed in her relationship with her mother-in-law she was overcome with a sense of guilt because she felt unable to 'love' her in what she supposed to be the only meaning of the word. Misunderstandings about belief – in other words bad theology – were a large part of her problem. The psychiatrist presented this case to a group of theologians and asked for their help and comments but most of them saw no relationship at all between theology, as they understood it, and the woman's original problem.

Not long ago I went to a meeting arranged by a church group on the subject of the Industrial Relations Act. In the debate a trades' unionist and an industrialist presented their cases from such entrenched positions that it seemed to rule out the possibility of any fresh thinking about human relations in industry. A clergyman attending the meeting commented to me – 'I cannot see what this has to do with the gospel'. His entire training and understanding of theology had made him unable to see how to make any contribution to a debate that was in desperate need of being opened up to a new level, a debate that had immediate bearing on how people treat each other, how the burden of the past is overcome and how justice is established, all of which are issues which should be central to Christian concern.

I believe that people in these situations need a better grasp of the gospel and a better understanding of God, and here theology has a very important role. Theology should help people to discriminate among the developments that are going on, to discern what things they should promote and what they should initiate in life. It should help them to see what to attack as being oppressive and obstructive to full human living. It should help people to understand what is involved in living as a Christian and as a member of the people of God.

My experience has shown me that in the kind of situations I have described clergy and lay people can feel, and be, very ineffective. I believe that, if theology is to play its proper part in changing this situation, there is urgent need for a new understanding of what theology is, what its purpose is and what is the best way for it to be engaged in and developed today.

1. What Theology Is

Theology is a continuing process in which a particular present situation and the gospel of God are seen to be related to each other.

It is the problem of the relationship of the two that makes continuous theological thinking necessary. It is serious attention to both that differentiates theological thinking from any other kind of thinking.

Present experience forces us to ask ultimate questions and acts as a spur to theological thinking. For this reason present experience can be an excellent – and some would say the very best – starting point of theology. I am myself at present working with a number of groups, which include all sorts of people, many of whom have little touch with the churches. But their interest in theology springs directly out of their lives and their deep concern about what is happening in the world.

Theological thinking is a perfectly normal human activity and does not need to be self-conscious, but as this point it may be useful to analyse its ingredients. *Diagram 5* overleaf gives an analysis of the kind of things that happen in a theological discussion, which may of course be of the most informal kind.

The diagram shows that theology is a continuous process in which present experience and the understanding of Christian faith confront each other, with the result that old ideas and old expressions must constantly be re-thought in the light of new experience and new questions.

The material of theology includes present experience (A) and the biblical data and what people have made of it (B). In order to give real weight to both, the theological process should be a joint effort in which people with different types of experience have a contribution to make as well as the academic theologian.

Theology does not provide prescriptive conclusions which determine *a priori* the final answers to the questions people raise. It does not in itself create faith. Its function is to help provide formulations of faith and in this way to help towards better Christian understanding, offering people theological expressions which enable them to take the next step in a continuous process of exploration.

The theological process is never finished for new experience constantly brings new questions as well as new knowledge,

Diagram 5

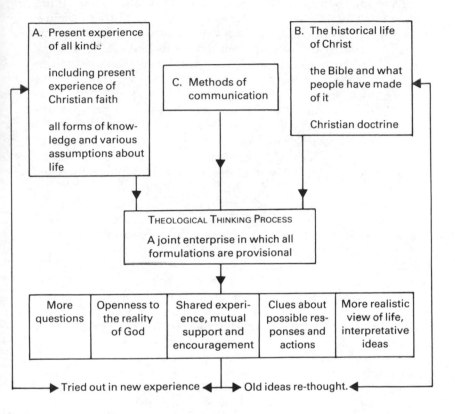

A. Present experience of all kinds

including present experience of Christian faith

all forms of knowledge and various assumptions about life

C. Methods of communication

B. The historical life of Christ

the Bible and what people have made of it

Christian doctrine

THEOLOGICAL THINKING PROCESS

A joint enterprise in which all formulations are provisional

| More questions | Openness to the reality of God | Shared experience, mutual support and encouragement | Clues about possible responses and actions | More realistic view of life, interpretative ideas |

Tried out in new experience ◄──► Old ideas re-thought. ◄

The operation of the whole is in the presence and power of the Holy Spirit.

opening up both the possibility and the need for new understandings.

The diagram is not meant to suggest a stereotyped method of working, but rather to provide a model of theological understanding. All sorts of methods are possible within this general understanding of what is happening when theology takes life situations seriously.

For example – a group of industrial managers meets monthly to work out the meaning of Christian faith for their lives in industry. At one point they analysed specific questions faced by individual

members. They then talked about the aspects of faith they felt to
have some bearing on these questions. This made them realize
their need for a better understanding of some of the basic themes
of Christian faith – such as sin, God, reconciliation. All the time
they are having to live with their questions and get on with the
job. Their meetings are very friendly informal affairs but never-
theless all the ingredients of theological thinking shown in the
diagram are present.

The programme of another group is planned so that one
meeting starts with a member introducing a question from his
own experience, while the next meeting starts with discussion of
a particular doctrine and its relevance to life. Each group finds the
approach that suits it best, and in the end each explores the same
territory.

The same process is spelt out in another context by C. F. D.
Moule in *The Birth of the New Testament*. He describes how parts
of the New Testament came into being: 'the guidance of the
spirit of God was granted not in the form of a code of behaviour nor of any written deposit of direction, but of inspired
insight. It was granted ad hoc to Christians as they met
together, confronting the immediate problems with the Gospel
behind them, the Holy Spirit among them, and the will to find
out the action required of the People of God in the near
future.'[2]

A major difference that stands out in our own day is that it is
not now possible or useful to define exactly who belongs and who
does not belong to the people of God. Theological discussion that
arises out of the concerns of daily life normally, as I have found,
involves a majority of non-church people, who find it natural to
discuss theological questions in the secular terms of contemporary culture. Only a minority will be familiar with the technical
terms that are used in churches. Both groups share a common
concern for such topics as justice, truth and the realization of the
full potential of human life. But the theological task is bedevilled
by the inability of the two groups to understand each other and
by the great difficulty of any kind of bridge building. If theology is
to be creative today a major task for the local congregation is to
help its members to be aware of the needs of the situation, and to
enable at least some of them to engage with theological
knowledge and understanding in an open type of discussion in
groups where secular people are asking questions in secular
terms.

2. The Purpose of Theology

The purpose of theology is to help people understand what is involved in living as a Christian and as a member of the people of God. It must do this in relation to the actual situations in which people live.

Hence theology is today having to rediscover its own identity and purpose. *Diagram 6* shows the three main aspects of Christian life: A – awareness of God, B – practical living in the world and C – theology which is the link between the other two. Theology must serve the two aspects A and B, and it is dead and useless if it loses touch with either of them. The task of theology is the responsibility of the church and as such it is always corporate and contextual. It has to help people understand what is involved in a living awareness of God and how to live in the world. In this way it has an accountability both to the church and to the world. It continues to be a living process in as far as it is sensitive to the concerns and questions arising in contemporary life and discerns the will of God for the present.

Diagram 6

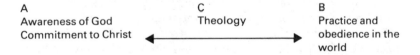

A	C	B
Awareness of God	Theology	Practice and
Commitment to Christ	←—————————→	obedience in the
		world

3. How Can Theology Be Worked Out

In practice today theology is done in three different settings – the universities, the church and the world. There are questions to be asked about what happens in each of these settings and their relationship to each other.

The universities are crucial because they employ the majority of academic theologians. Their resources are vital to theological advance in any setting.

At a theological conference at Bossey in August, a number of leading scientists were present for the purpose of stimulating an inter-disciplinary discussion involving theologians, biologists, psychologists, psychiatrists and others. For many this was their first experience of such a dialogue – yet the meaning and destiny of man's life needs to be understood in relation to data provided by science with all the new questions and possibilities it raises. This kind of conversation should be taking place in all universities. Many students begin to ask questions when they come to university, and there is desperate need for the universities to stimulate open and cross-disciplinary discussion on the major questions which society faces. I believe it is the role of theologians to start discussions within the university and beyond on questions about the responsibility of science, the relationship of rich and poor nations, unemployment and economic policies and all the changes in culture and leisure.

The church should be initiating the same kind of discussion in all sorts of settings. As a contribution to this process, one aspect of my job is to identify the main concerns of people in the North-East Region. These include technological change, long term unemployment and the social disruption epitomized in the Category 'D' villages, the lack of creative political thought in local government, educational and cultural deficiences. I am also aware of the immense potential of creativity illustrated by some of the planning and development in the region.

Theology has a contribution to make to all these questions. Some further practical implications must be underlined.

This approach to theology makes it essential that clergy and laity work together. I have been present when clergy have talked with people working in industry, in the social services or local government and I have noted how stimulated they were by the discussion. Several of the clergy have said: 'I wish all our discussions could be done in company with lay people.' I believe it should be the norm for clergy and laity to study and plan together. Why is this not happening at the level of the congregation? And why is it that the discussions that do take place are so often confined to secondary matters to the exclusion of the main questions of concern to the rest of the world?

Lay people as well as clergy must learn to work in a secular style for they will normally be engaged in dialogue with non-church people. Such a style is the basis of what has been described as 'frontier' work, a concept that should be spelt out in some detail. It was Dr J. H. Oldham who gave the idea currency when he started the Frontier Council in the 1940s. Although much of his work has been misunderstood or forgotten, creative frontier work continues to be done – for example by industrial missions, by some social responsibility groups, by ad hoc groups working on particular issues and by the kind of local groups that have emerged from the Teesside urban ministry programmes.

A ministry that addresses itself to the world's concerns raises questions for the theological colleges and for the training of clergy in general. The role of the clergy is increasingly that of enabling lay people to perform their own ministry in the world, and also of helping congregations to give both the general and the particular support that is needed for such a ministry. This closer integration into one ministry that includes the whole church means that clergy need to share more fully in the thought and lives of lay people. Church lay people also need to open up their thinking. I believe there is a real possibility that, when clergy and lay people work together, there will be a mutual breaking down of closed thinking.

If clergy are to be equipped for this new relationship and role their training must include the following essentials:

1. Knowledge of modern society and the situations people face in the four main areas of life – where they live, where they work, where they exercise social and political responsibility and where they develop their talents (particularly in education, leisure and culture).

2. Knowledge of the Bible and what people have made of it, knowledge of Christian doctrine and Christian controversy and an understanding of the church's task and mission.

3. Skills in relating life situations and the gospel ((1) and (2) above) and opportunities to develop the ability to share in a joint task.

At present training is concentrated on the academic aspect of theology (2) and the examinations connected with it.

In the theological colleges a small but increasing amount of time has been added to an already full time-table in order to introduce students to aspects of modern society (1). This is seldom done on the basis of a sociological or theological analysis of modern society, but tends to be 'inspirational' and dependent on the availability of 'field-work' openings. For instance, it is easier to attach a student to a caring institution than to put him into a situation where larger questions about the direction of society must be asked.

Hardly any time is allocated to acquiring the skills required to relate the gospel to actual situations of life (3), with the result that gospel and life ((1) and (2)) are seen as separate entities and the significance of both is lost. The theme of this essay is that theology must be integral to life. It is not a matter of putting more things into the syllabus, but of planning for disciplined reflection that relates actual issues arising in the practical work to the main Christian themes that are studied in the academic course. If students learn to think theologically about day to day issues during their training, there is a chance that they will continue to do so during the rest of their ministry. In-service training will be of help here, but it needs a foundation upon which to build.

The practical issues that emerge for theological training have led to some radical experiments in which much of the training takes place away from the theological colleges. For instance in the Ripon Hall-Morden Project, students live and work during part of their training in the Morden area, where theological thinking can be done in relation to practical involvement and with the same people. There is room for a serious development of this kind in the North East.

A great deal of creative work is going on in this region on the lines I have described in this article. Further experiment is not what is wanted, but long term planning backed by the necessary financial, theological and other resources to develop work that is already going on. There are, for instance, proposals for a Christian Urban Exploration Scheme, which would draw together and develop the large amount of 'frontier' work that has been going on over a number of years in Teesside. Something of the kind is clearly needed for the whole North East region.

After the war the church in Germany recognized the size of the task it faced if it was to give people encouragement and vision for re-building a way of life. The German Academies were the practical outcome of this understanding and determination. The Academies created a new style of Christian ministry and made a significant contribution to the life of post-war Germany. It was Hitler and the war that forced German Christians to re-think their faith and act on their conclusions. Can we respond likewise to the challenge of our times and make the same sort of impact upon our situation?

Notes

Notes

Chapter I How God got Hold of Me

1. Margaret Kane, *Gospel in Industrial Society*, SCM Press 1980, p. 1.
2. Abbe Michonneau, *Revolution in a City Parish*, Blackfriars 1949, pp. 2, 7.
3. Maisie Ward, *France Pagan?*, Sheed and Ward 1949, p. 74.
4. Ibid., p. 112.
5. Michonneau, op. cit., p. 2.
6. See *Strategist for the Spirit – Leslie Hunter Bishop of Sheffield 1939–62*, ed., Gordon Hewitt, Becket Publications 1985.
7. Thomas Weiser (ed.), *Planning for Mission*, Epworth Press 1966, 'Zonal Structures for the Church', pp. 208 ff.
8. The North-East Region is the area bounded in the North by the Tweed, in the South by the Humber, on the East by the sea and in the West by the Pennine Range. It is not officially designated as a region and is to be distinguished from the Northern Region which includes the Counties of Northumberland, Tyne and Wear, Durham, Cleveland *and* Cumbria. Ecclesiastically (and I had to take note of ecclesiastical as well as secular structures), the North East includes the Anglican Dioceses of Newcastle, Durham and York and the two Roman Catholic Dioceses of Hexham and Newcastle and Middlesbrough.
9. Margaret Kane, *Theology in an Industrial Society*, SCM Press 1975, see pp. 55 ff.; *Gospel in Industrial Society*, SCM Press 1980, see pp. 28 ff.
10. *Gospel in Industrial Society*, p. 37.
11. Ibid., p. 31.
12. Ibid., p. 31.
13. These figures, but not the comment, are based on *The State of the Region Report 1984* produced by the North of England County Councils' Association, and a summary of the report made by Canon W. H. Wright.
14. David E. Jenkins was consecrated Bishop of Durham in July 1984; Robert Moore is Professor of Sociology, Aberdeen University; John Loftus died in January 1981.

Chapter II What God has Taught Me

1. Some other religions have their own theology. Here I confine myself to Christian theology.

Chapter III Conflicting Patterns of Belief

1. For more on models see I. T. Ramsey, *Religious Language*, SCM Press 1957; *Models for Divine Activity*, SCM Press 1973.
2. This diagram is based on a model in *Diagrammatic Modelling*, The William Temple Foundation, Occasional Papers Number 4, 1980, pp. 34, 35.
3. Ibid., pp. 33, 34.
4. E. Schillebeeckx, *Jesus*, Collins, Fount edition 1983, pp. 141–2.

Chapter IV   God and World

1. 'Technology is a complex matter of scientific method (observation, hypothesis, test or verification) applied to the development of tools and their application to the human and material environment. It has three elements: attitudes, tools and techniques and organization. These factors react upon each other' ('Technology and War', Professor James O'Connell reproduced in Southwell Papers 1983).
2. Bishop's Letter, 15 November 1941.
3. Rt Rev. E. R. Wickham, Chairman Churches Working Group, Industry Year 1986.
4. Martin Wright in reply to the foregoing statement by Rt Rev. E. R. Wickham.
5. *Towards the Conversion of England*, Report of a Committee on Evangelism appointed by the Archbishops of Canterbury and York, Press and Publications Board of the Church Assembly 1945.
6. *Change*, Hong Kong Industrial Committee, April 1984.

Chapter V   Church and World

1. In the local Government Re-organization of 1974 Tyne and Wear became a Metropolitan County.
2. *Faith in the City*, Church House Publishing 1985 (ACUPA).
3. *Faith in the City* emphasizes the fact that many council housing estates, although they do not share all the official indicators of deprivation, should be treated as Urban Priority Areas.
4. Ibid., p. 33, para. 2.25: National average church attendance in each parish = 1.4% of parish population; UPA average church attendance in each parish = .85% of parish population.
5. Richard Niebuhr, *Christ and Culture*, Faber and Faber 1952.
6. The need was not entirely lost sight of for a Sunderland Institute of Christian Education later started and ran a number of courses each year.
7. Paper by M. Kane for Middlesborough Deanery Planning Committee.

Chapter VI   Good News to the Poor?

1. Jose Miguez Bonino, *Revolutionary Theology Come of Age*, SPCK 1975, pp. 166–7.
2. Ibid., p. 167.
3. ACUPA emphasizes the need to address the issue of powerlessness in the UPAs: p. 197, para. 8.76.
4. The model I had in mind was that of Horst Symanovski of Gossner Mission in Germany. Between 1950 and 1954 he did intermittent labouring in a large cement works, while at the same time making a home for young industrial workers. It was this combination of labouring work and creating a Christian centre that enabled him to maintain touch with the lives and thoughts of manual workers. The jobs he did were of a casual nature that made it possible to drop in and out of work and thus to have time to develop the centre and its mission. Horst Symanovski, *The Christian in an Industrial Society*, Collins 1964.
5. V.S.-B., Report to Teesside Industrial Mission.
6. Michael Crick, *Scargill and the Miners*, Penguin Books 1985.
7. Gustavo Gutierrez, *We Drink from Our Own Wells*, SCM Press 1984, for example.
8. ACUPA, p. 62, para 3.29. The report here refers especially to the Christian poor, but we need also to learn from the *un*-Christian poor.
9. Reinhold Niebuhr, *Moral Man and Immoral Society*, Scribner 1932.

Chapter VII   Theology for Everyone

1. For a more detailed discussion of the differences between these theologies see my *Theology in an Industrial Society*, Chapter III, 'Theology – The Continuing Search for Meaning'.
2. ACUPA makes the same point, p. 66, para. 3.39.
3. *All Are Called: Towards a Theology of the Laity*, Essays from a Working Party of the General Synod Board of Education, CIO 1985 'Clericalism, Clergy and Laity', A. O. Dyson, p. 16.
4. R. Etchells, unpublished paper.
5. *All Are Called*, Dyson, p. 16.
6. J. L. Segundo, *The Liberation of Theology*, Gill and MacMillan 1977, pp. 7–9.
7. 'Academy Style Services in the North East Region', unpublished paper by Margaret Kane, 1972.
8. Certificate in Religious Studies (by thesis), William Temple Foundation/ Manchester University; MA/Diploma in Theology, 'Theological Understanding of Industrial Society', University of Hull, Department of Theology.
9. This vision has now taken shape in the Marygate Francis Dewar Project.
10. Margaret Kane's notes on meeting 31 October 1976.

Chapter VIII   Alternative Church Structures

1. Bruce M. Cooper, Joseph Rimmer and Malcolm J. Sweeting, *Structuring the Church for Mission*, Belton Books 1969.
2. *The Teesplan   Teesside Survey and Plan*, HMSO 1969.
3. 'Respond' was formed as a result of a report presented in 1983 by a 'Think Tank' to an ecumenical group of senior church leaders on 'The Role and Response of the Church to Cleveland's Industrial Crisis'. Its aim is to encourage new and positive ideas about Cleveland's problems and opportunities. And to turn such ideas into action!
4. *The Link*, Newcastle Diocesan News, May 1975.
5. *Theological Training: A Policy for the Future*, GS Misc. 57.
6. Archbishop Donald Coggan.
7. 'Proposed Institute of Christian Education' unpublished paper, Margaret Kane, May 1977.
8. Professor S. W. Sykes, 'A Proposal concerning the use of money available to the Trustees of the College of St Hild and St Bede in the event of a merger with the University of Durham', November 1977.
9. John Tiller, *A Strategy for the Church's Ministry*, CIO Publishing 1983.
10. ACUPA, p. 70, para. 3.45.

Chapter IX   What Kind of God?

1. Jon Sobrino, *Christianity at the Crossroads*, SCM Press 1978, p. 9.
2. In September 1984 York Minster was struck by lightning and the ensuing fire caused considerable structural damage. Those who disapproved of the theology of the Bishop of Durham, Rt Rev. D. E. Jenkins, saw this as an act of God, by which he had shown his judgment on the Bishop and those who had consecrated him in the Minster a few days before the fire.
3. 'Belief in God Today', T. A. Baker unpublished paper 1983.

Chapter X   Journeying On

1. Charles Davis, *God's Grace in History*, Collins, Fontana Books 1966, p. 42.

2. Schillebeeckx, *Jesus*, p. 671.

3. Dietrich Bonhoeffer, *Letters and Papers from Prison*, Enlarged edition, SCM Press 1971, 'Christians and Pagans', p. 349.

Appendix II   Secular Experience and Theological Thinking

1. Parts of this Appendix were presented to a Conference on 'Contextual or Dogmatic Theology?' arranged by the World Council of Churches at Bossey in August 1971. In a note to the present essay when it was used for the consultation in December 1971, Ian Ramsey wrote: 'Margaret Kane is my theological consultant in industrial and social affairs and is working ecumenically throughout the area that goes beyond the Diocese to cover both sides of the Tyne and Tees. Her task is to help provide a background of theological thinking that can support the churches' attempts to present the gospel in a way that speaks to the specific needs of the North East and its people.'

2. C. F. D. Moule, *The Birth of the New Testament*, A. & C. Black 1962, p. 212.

Index

Index

Ushaw College, 91, 94

Whitby, Bishop of, 107
Women, 74, 90, 96, 106, 138; at work, 69–72; in ministry, 5, 71ff., 116, 136
World, 56f., 116f.

York, Diocese, 10, 54